CONGRESSIONAL POLICIES, PRACTICES AND PROCEDURES

INTERNATIONAL SOCIAL SECURITY: AGREEMENTS AND SELECT RETIREMENT COMPARISONS

Congressional Policies, Practices and Procedures

Additional books in this series can be found on Nova's website under the Series tab.

Additional E-books in this series can be found on Nova's website under the E-books tab.

American Political, Economic, and Security Issues

Additional books in this series can be found on Nova's website under the Series tab.

Additional E-books in this series can be found on Nova's website under the E-books tab.

CONGRESSIONAL POLICIES, PRACTICES AND PROCEDURES

INTERNATIONAL SOCIAL SECURITY: AGREEMENTS AND SELECT RETIREMENT COMPARISONS

NICOLE E. PAMPINO
EDITOR

Nova Science Publishers, Inc.
New York

For permission to use material from this book please contact us:
Telephone 631-231-7269; Fax 631-231-8175
Web Site: http://www.novapublishers.com

LIBRARY OF CONGRESS CATALOGING-IN-PUBLICATION DATA

International social security : agreements and select retirement comparisons
/ editors, Nicole E. Pampino.
p. cm.
Includes index.
Includes reprints of reports originally published by the Social Security
Administration.
ISBN 978-1-61761-430-9 (hbk.)
1. Social security. 2. Old age pensions. 3. Retirement income. I.
Pampino, Nicole E. II. United States. Social Security Administration.
HD7091.I646 2010
368.4'3--dc22
2010028632

Published by Nova Science Publishers, Inc. † New York

CONTENTS

PREFACE

International Social Security agreements are bilateral agreements primarily intended to eliminate dual Social Security taxation based on the same work and provide benefit protection for workers who divide their careers between the United States and a foreign country. Most jobs in the United States are covered by Social Security. The Social Security Act extends Social Security coverage to all U.S. citizens and resident aliens who are employed abroad by U.S. companies as well as those who are self-employed in a foreign country. This book provides an overview of the purpose and operation of international Social Security agreements and discusses the effects of agreements on selected provisions of the Social Security Act while addressing some concerns raised by policymakers about the agreements.

Chapter 1- International Social Security agreements are bilateral agreements primarily intended to eliminate dual Social Security taxation based on the same work and provide benefit protection for workers who divide their careers between the United States and a foreign country. Most jobs in the United States are covered by Social Security. In addition, the Social Security Act extends Social Security coverage to U.S. citizens and resident aliens who are employed abroad by U.S. companies as well as those who are self-employed in a foreign country. Generally, a U.S. worker abroad and his or her employer would be required to contribute both to the U.S. Social Security system and the Social Security system of the country where the work is performed based on the same work. International agreements eliminate dual Social Security taxation in these circumstances by allowing workers and their employers to contribute to only one Social Security system (either the U.S. or the foreign system depending on the terms of the agreement). In addition, international agreements allow workers who divide their careers between the

United States and a foreign country to fill gaps in Social Security coverage by combining work credits under each country's system to qualify for benefits under one or both systems. If a worker qualifies for benefits based on combined (totalized) work credits, the benefit payable under either system is prorated to take into account the actual period during which the worker was covered by that system.

Chapter 2- When we say you are outside the United States, we mean you are not in one of the 50 states, the District of Columbia, Puerto Rico, the U.S. Virgin Islands, Guam, the Northern Mariana Islands or American Samoa. Once you have been out of the U.S. for at least 30 days in a row, you are considered to be outside the country until you return and stay in the U.S. for at least 30 days in a row. If you are not a U.S. citizen, you also may have to prove that you were lawfully present in the United States for that 30-day period. For more information, contact the nearest U.S. Embassy, consulate or Social Security office.

Chapter 3- Recently various analysts have called attention to the apparent success of the Canadian social assistance system in reducing poverty among the elderly and have suggested that there may be lessons to be drawn from the Canadian experience that are relevant to the evolution of the U.S. Supplemental Security Income (SSI) program. This article profiles the Canadian system, compares the system to the U.S. SSI program, reviews the consequences for elderly poverty rates, assesses system costs, and then comments on pertinence of the Canadian experience to SSI policy. The Canadian minimum income guarantee for the elderly is substantially more generous than what is provided by the United States, but it is misleading to claim that the Canadian system costs only "slightly more" than the U.S. program. Such a judgment overlooks a key and costly part of the Canadian system, the Old Age Security demogrant. We estimate the total costs to Canada of providing income support for elderly persons receiving a Guaranteed Income Supplement (GIS) in 2004 to be approximately C$ 13.3 billion (roughly US$11.1 billion), slightly more than 1 percent of gross domestic product (GDP) and almost *fourteen times* the U.S. allocation for SSI and food stamps for elderly SSI recipients. The significance of this commitment is underscored when it is recognized that in 2004 Canadian GDP per capita was just 80 percent of the U.S. level. The Canadian example suggests U.S. policymakers consider better integration of SSI with basic Social Security benefits, experimenting with alternatives to restricting SSI eligibility to individuals with very few assets, and reducing barriers to program access.

Chapter 4- In 1981, Chile introduced a new system of privately managed individual accounts, also called capitalization, replacing its public pay-as-you-go pension system (PAYG). Since 1990, 10 other countries in the region have adopted some form of what has become known as the "Chilean model": Argentina (1994), Bolivia (1997), Colombia (1993), Costa Rica (1995), Dominican Republic (2003), El Salvador (1998), Mexico (1997), Panama (2008), Peru (1993), and Uruguay (1996).

Over the years, Chile made some major changes to its capitalization system, such as liberalizing investment rules and increasing the type and number of pension funds that a pension fund management company (AFP) must offer its account holders. However, despite these and other changes, a number of policy challenges remain unresolved including large groups of workers who are not covered and irregular worker participation rates, both of which could lead to inadequate retirement benefits. Also, according to international standards, the administrative fees the AFPs are charging account holders are high and could significantly decrease the size of a worker's pension.

Chapter 5- Since July 1, 2007, New Zealanders have had a new option for their retirement savings—KiwiSaver—a type of subsidized, defined contribution retirement savings plan offered by private-sector providers. New labor force entrants in permanent positions who are aged 18 or older are automatically enrolled in a KiwiSaver plan, but are able to opt out of the plan if they wish. Also, all individuals younger than age 65, including anyone not in the labor force, are permitted to set up a KiwiSaver account.

Chapter 6- This article examines the development of Japanese voluntary employer-sponsored retirement plans with an emphasis on recent trends. Until 2001, companies in Japan offered retirement benefits as lump-sum severance payments and/or benefits from one of two types of defined benefit (DB) pension plans. One type of DB plan was based on the occupational pension model used in the United States before the adoption of the Employee Retirement Income Security Act of 1974 (ERISA), but lacked the funding, vesting, and other protective features contained in ERISA. The other type of DB plan allowed companies to opt out of the earnings-related portion of social security, commonly referred to as "contracting out."

In: International Social Security: Agreements… ISBN: 978-1-61761-430-9
Editors: Nicole E. Pampino

Chapter 1

INTERNATIONAL SOCIAL SECURITY AGREEMENTS

Dawn Nuschler

SUMMARY

International Social Security agreements are bilateral agreements primarily intended to eliminate dual Social Security taxation based on the same work and provide benefit protection for workers who divide their careers between the United States and a foreign country. Most jobs in the United States are covered by Social Security. In addition, the Social Security Act extends Social Security coverage to U.S. citizens and resident aliens who are employed abroad by U.S. companies as well as those who are self-employed in a foreign country. Generally, a U.S. worker abroad and his or her employer would be required to contribute both to the U.S. Social Security system and the Social Security system of the country where the work is performed based on the same work. International agreements eliminate dual Social Security taxation in these circumstances by allowing workers and their employers to contribute to only one Social Security system (either the U.S. or the foreign system depending on the terms of the agreement). In addition, international agreements allow workers who divide their careers between the United States and a foreign country to fill gaps in Social Security coverage by combining work credits under each country's system to qualify for benefits under one or both systems. If a worker qualifies for benefits based on combined (totalized) work credits, the benefit payable under either system is prorated to take into account the actual period during which the worker was covered by that system.

By eliminating dual Social Security taxation, international agreements reduce the cost of doing business abroad. As a result, they can affect the competitiveness and profitability of U.S. companies with foreign operations and promote investment in the United States by foreign companies. In addition, international agreements affect the application of certain provisions of the Social Security Act, including the alien nonpayment provision. The alien nonpayment provision places restrictions on the payment of U.S. Social Security benefits to noncitizens who reside outside the United States, with broad exceptions. These payment restrictions may be waived for beneficiaries who are residents of a country with which the United States has an agreement.

Since 1977, the President has had the authority to negotiate Social Security agreements with foreign countries. Currently, there are 24 Social Security agreements in force. Another agreement (with Mexico) has been signed, but is not in force. In December 2007, about $28 million was paid in monthly benefits to about 146,200 recipients under U.S. Social Security agreements.

Many observers agree that international Social Security agreements can be beneficial for U.S. companies and workers. However, some policymakers have expressed concerns about the agreements. Because the agreements impose a cost to the U.S. Social Security system, some policymakers point to the need for greater assurances that the data relied upon by the United States to administer the agreements are complete and accurate, a condition necessary to protect the Social Security trust funds from improper payments. In addition, they point to concerns about the role of Congress in the approval process for potential agreements, as well as the need for enhanced reporting requirements and periodic evaluation of agreements in force. These and other concerns are reflected in legislative proposals such as S. 42 and H.R. 132 in the 111th Congress.

This chapter provides an overview of the purpose and operation of international Social Security agreements. In addition, it provides a discussion of the effects of agreements on selected provisions of the Social Security Act and concerns raised by some policymakers about the agreements.

INTRODUCTION

International Social Security agreements are bilateral agreements primarily intended to eliminate dual Social Security taxation based on the same work and provide benefit protection for workers who divide their careers between the United States and a foreign country. By eliminating dual Social Security taxation, the agreements reduce the cost of doing business abroad. In turn, they can affect the competitiveness and profitability of U.S. companies with foreign operations as well as promote investment in the United States by foreign companies. Social Security agreements also affect the application of certain provisions of the Social Security Act, such as the alien nonpayment provision which places restrictions on the payment of U.S. Social Security benefits to noncitizens residing outside the United States, with broad exceptions.[1]

Since 1977, the President has had the authority to negotiate Social Security agreements with foreign countries (pursuant to Section 233 of the Social Security Act). Currently, there are 24 Social Security agreements in force (see Table 2 for a list of U.S. Social Security agreements in force). Another agreement (with Mexico) has been signed, but is not in force.

This chapter provides an overview of the purpose and operation of international Social Security agreements.[2] It also provides a discussion of the effects of agreements on selected provisions of the Social Security Act and concerns raised by some policymakers about the agreements.[3]

MAIN PURPOSES

Eliminating Dual Social Security Taxation

One of the main purposes of international Social Security agreements is to eliminate dual Social Security taxation. Dual Social Security taxation occurs when a worker from one country is employed or self-employed in another country and both countries require that contributions be paid on the same work. In the United States, Social Security-covered workers and their employers each pay 6.2% of earnings up to $106,800 (in 2010) in Social Security payroll taxes.[4] Workers who are self-employed pay 12.4% of net self-employment income up to $106,800, and they may deduct one-half of payroll taxes from federal income taxes.

Most jobs in the United States[5] (whether performed by U.S. citizens or noncitizens) are covered by Social Security.[6] The Social Security Administration (SSA) estimates that 94% of workers in paid employment or self-employment in the United States are covered by Social Security.[7] Workers who are *not* covered by Social Security include

(1) state and local government workers participating in alternative retirement systems;
(2) election workers earning less than $1,500 in 2010;
(3) ministers who choose not to be covered and certain religious sects;
(4) federal government workers hired before 1984 (elected office holders, political appointees and judges are mandatorily covered regardless of when their service began);
(5) college students working at their academic institutions;
(6) household workers earning less than $1,700 in 2010, or those under age 18 for whom household work is not their principal occupation;
(7) self-employed workers with annual net earnings below $400;
(8) foreign students and exchange visitors who hold F-1, J-1, M-1, Q1 and Q2 visas if the work is performed in connection with their studies or for the purpose of their visit to the United States (J-1 visa holders who are in the United States for 18 months or longer are required to pay Social Security payroll taxes); and
(9) foreign agricultural workers who hold H-2A visas.

The Social Security Act also extends Social Security coverage to U.S. citizens and residents who are employed abroad by U.S. companies (such as in a branch office located in a foreign country).[8] As a result, a U.S. worker and his or her employer generally would be required to contribute both to the U.S. Social Security system and the Social Security system of the country where the work is performed. In addition, U.S. citizens and residents who are employed by a foreign affiliate of a U.S. company are subject to dual taxation if the company has entered into an agreement with the U.S. Department of the Treasury, Internal Revenue Service, under Section 3 121(l) of the Internal Revenue Code to provide U.S. Social Security coverage for employees of a foreign affiliate.

In some cases, a U.S. company that sends an employee to work in a foreign country may agree to pay both the employee's and the employer's shares of the Social Security tax under the foreign system. Payment of the employee's share of the Social Security tax by the employer may be considered taxable compensation to the employee, thereby increasing the employee's income tax liability. The employer may also agree to pay the additional income taxes on behalf of the employee. SSA estimates that, in some countries, an employer's foreign Social Security costs can be as much as 65% to 70% of the employee's salary when foreign Social Security taxes and additional income taxes paid by the employer on behalf of the employee are taken into account.[9]

In addition, the Social Security Act extends Social Security coverage to U.S. citizens and residents who are self-employed in a foreign country. As a result, self-employed workers abroad are also affected by dual Social Security taxation.

International agreements eliminate dual taxation on the same earnings by requiring workers and their employers to contribute to only one Social Security system based on the coverage provisions of the agreements. Each agreement includes coverage rules that determine whether a person's work is covered under the Social Security system of the sending country or that of the foreign country.[10] Under the agreements, there are basic rules of coverage that apply to workers who are sent by an employer to work abroad as well as self-employed workers (see rules regarding the self-employed). In addition, there are special rules and exceptions that apply allowing for variation in the rules of coverage under each agreement.[11]

The basic rule of coverage under international agreements is the *territoriality rule*, which specifies that a worker is covered under the Social Security system of the country where the work is performed, unless the agreement provides for one or more exceptions. Generally, exceptions are provided to "ensure that a worker is covered under the system of the country to which he or she has the more direct connection."[12] A primary exception to the territoriality rule is the *detached worker rule*. Under this rule, a person who is sent by an employer to work in a foreign country on a temporary basis (generally *five years or less*) would continue to be covered under the sending country's system and would be exempt from coverage under the foreign system. Conversely, a person who is sent by an employer to work in a foreign country *for more than five years* would be covered under the foreign system and would be exempt from coverage under the sending country's system. The basic rules of coverage are summarized in Table 1.

Table 1. Basic Rules of Coverage Under International Social Security Agreements

Rule	Brief Description
Territoriality Rule	A person is covered under the Social Security system of the country in which the work is performed.
Detached Worker Rule	A person sent by an employer to work in a foreign country on a temporary basis (generally 5 years or less) will continue to be covered under the sending country's Social Security system and will be exempt from coverage under the foreign system.
	Conversely, a person sent by an employer to work in a foreign country for *more than 5 years* will be covered under the foreign system and will be exempt from coverage under the sending country's system.
Nationality Rule	A person is covered under the Social Security system of his or her country of nationality.
	This coverage rule applies only under the agreement with Italy.
Residence Rule	A person is covered under the Social Security system of the country in which he or she resides.
	This coverage rule generally applies to self-employment.

Source: Information based on the Social Security Administration's Program Operations Manual System (POMS), Section RS 020 (Coverage Under International Agreements), available at *http://policy.ssa.gov/poms.nsf/links/0302000000.*

Notes: Special exceptions may apply under some agreements and rules of coverage may differ for government employees and other categories of workers.

For example, if a U.S. worker is sent by an employer to work in Canada and the assignment is expected to last five years or less, he or she would remain covered under the U.S. Social Security system. The worker and his or her employer would be required to contribute only to the U.S. system. Alternatively, if a U.S. worker is sent by an employer to work in Canada and the assignment is expected to last for more than five years, he or she would be covered only under the Canadian Social Security system. The worker and his or her employer would be required to contribute only to the Canadian system. Thus, the detached worker rule allows workers and their employers to avoid paying Social Security payroll taxes under two systems based on the same earnings and minimizes disruptions in Social Security coverage for workers who are transferred abroad on temporary assignments.

The agreement with Italy is unique in that the primary exception to the territoriality rule is the *nationality rule*, which specifies that a worker is covered under the Social Security system of his or her country of nationality.[13] For example, if an Italian worker is sent by an employer to work in the United States, he or she would remain covered under the Italian Social Security system, regardless of the period of employment in the United States.[14]

Generally, different coverage rules apply to *self-employed* workers. Under most agreements, the general rule of coverage for self-employed workers is the *residence rule*, which specifies that a person is covered under the Social Security system of the country in which he or she resides. For example, under the agreement with Switzerland, a Swiss citizen who resides in the United States and is self-employed is covered under the U.S. system and exempt from coverage under the Swiss system.

Some agreements, such as those with Belgium, France, Germany, Italy and Japan, use other primary rules of coverage for self-employment. For example, under the agreement with Belgium, a self-employed worker is subject to the territoriality rule if he or she conducts business in only one country and the residence rule if he or she conducts business in both countries.[15] Under the agreement with Germany, the basic rule of coverage for both employees and self-employed workers is the territoriality rule, with exceptions provided, such as those under the detached worker rule.[16]

Filling Gaps in Social Security Coverage

The second main purpose of international Social Security agreements is to allow workers who divide their careers between the United States and a foreign country to fill gaps in Social Security coverage by combining work credits under each country's system to qualify for benefits under one or both systems. In the United States, a worker must have at least 6 quarters of coverage under the U.S. system (the person must have worked in the United States in Social Security- covered employment for at least 1½ years) to combine U.S. and foreign work credits.[17] This feature of international agreements allows workers who do not meet the minimum coverage requirements under either country's system potentially to qualify for *partial* benefits under one or both systems. If a worker qualifies for benefits based on combined (totalized) work credits, the benefit payable under either system is prorated to take into account the actual period during which the worker was covered by that system.[18]

For example, under the U.S. system, a worker generally needs 40 quarters (10 years) of Social Security-covered employment to be eligible for retirement benefits.[19] Because the United States and Canada have entered into an agreement, a U.S. worker who has five years of coverage under the U.S. system and five years of coverage under the Canadian system can meet the minimum coverage requirement for a U.S. Social Security retirement benefit based on combined coverage credits from the U.S. and Canada. The benefit would be prorated to reflect that the worker contributed to the U.S. system for only five years. In the absence of an agreement between the United States and Canada, the worker in this example would not be able to qualify for a retirement benefit under the U.S. system (nor would a U.S. citizen who had worked in Canada be eligible for benefits under the Canadian system).

Workers may also qualify for Social Security Disability Insurance (SSDI) benefits based on combined work credits. To qualify for SSDI benefits under the U.S. system, a worker must meet the definition of disability,[20] as well as a *recent work test* and a *duration of work test*. Under the recent work test, a worker must have earned a certain number of work credits within a specified period. The requirements vary depending on the age of the worker at the time he or she became disabled. For example, a worker who becomes disabled before the age of 24 must have 1½ years of Social Security-covered employment during the three-year period before the disability began. By comparison, a worker who becomes disabled at the age of 31 or later must have five years of Social Security-covered employment during the 10-year period before the disability began. Under the duration of work test, a worker must have a certain number of *total* work credits, which may have been earned at any time. The requirements vary depending on the age of the worker at the time he or she became disabled. For example, a worker who becomes disabled before the age of 28 must have a total of 1 ½ years of Social Security-covered employment, while a worker who becomes disabled at the age of 60 must have a total of 9½ years of Social Security-covered employment.[21] In any case, a worker must have at least 6 work credits (1½ years of Social Security-covered employment) to qualify for SSDI benefits, the same minimum number of credits needed under the U.S. system to combine U.S. and foreign work credits under the terms of an international agreement.

The ability to combine coverage credits under the U.S. system and a foreign system provides workers (and their family members) an opportunity to qualify for benefits under one or both systems that would not be payable otherwise because the worker did not work long enough or recently enough to meet the minimum coverage requirements. In this way, a worker's Social Security contributions are not "lost" to the system.[22]

Other Goals

By eliminating dual Social Security taxation, international agreements reduce the cost of doing business abroad. In doing so, they can affect the competitiveness and profitability of U.S. companies with foreign operations and promote investment in the United States by foreign companies. In addition, international agreements affect the application of certain provisions of the Social Security Act, including the alien nonpayment provision. The alien nonpayment provision places restrictions on the payment of U.S. Social Security benefits to noncitizens who reside outside the United States, with broad exceptions. These payment restrictions may be waived for beneficiaries who are residents of a country with which the United States has a Social Security agreement.[23] Supporters of international Social Security agreements point out that the waiver of residency requirements increases the portability of Social Security benefits for U.S. citizens and foreign nationals.

Negotiation, Congressional Review, and Implementation

Nature and Authority

International Social Security agreements are conducted and approved using the *executive agreement* method rather than the treaty process. Under U.S. law, there are four types of international agreements: (1) treaties, (2) sole executive agreements, (3) agreements pursuant to treaty, and (4) congressional-executive agreements.[24] Congressional-executive agreements are those that are authorized or approved by Congress, or both. International Social Security agreements fall into the fourth category because they are authorized by Congress in the Social Security Act. In addition, Congress has established in the statute a role for itself in reviewing these agreements.

The *Congressional Record* does not provide a discussion of why Congress chose the congressional-executive method over the treaty method for totalization agreements in 1977. However, some discussion of the approval method for totalization agreements occurred during a 1976 hearing before the House Ways and Means Social Security Subcommittee on H.R. 14429, the International Social Security Agreements Act, as described in the next section. A discussion of the characteristics of congressional-executive agreements may shed additional light on the matter. One feature of congressional-executive agreements is that they rely on an *ex ante* authorization by Congress, in which Congress has the opportunity to establish by law certain terms related to such agreements. With respect to Social Security agreements, Section 233 of the Social Security Act authorizes the President to enter into such agreements with foreign countries, establishes the congressional review process for the agreements and specifies reporting requirements. In addition, congressional-executive agreements usually contain an *ex post* approval mechanism that provides an opportunity for both houses of Congress (not just the Senate) to approve or reject an agreement. With respect to Social Security agreements, Section 233(e)(2) of the Social Security Act specifies that an agreement shall become effective after a period of 60 days during which the House of Representatives or the Senate is in session (i.e., a period of 60 session days) after an agreement is transmitted to Congress unless the House of Representatives or the Senate adopts a resolution of disapproval.[25]

Legislative History of Section 233 of the Social Security Act

According to congressional testimony by the Commissioner of Social Security in 1976, initial efforts in the United States toward totalization agreements with foreign countries can be found in the Supplementary Agreement to the 1948 Treaty of Friendship, Commerce and Navigation between the United States and Italy. In his statement, Commissioner James B. Cardwell indicated:

> Under the Supplementary Agreement, which became effective in 1961, both countries declared their adherence to a policy of preventing gaps in social security protection by permitting periods of social security coverage in both countries to be counted in determining benefit rights in both countries.[26]

The Supplementary Agreement was signed by the United States and Italy in 1951 and ratified by the U.S. Senate in 1953.[27] While the Supplementary Agreement provided for the negotiation of a totalization agreement between the parties (referred to in the Supplementary Agreement as an “arrangement”), the Senate ratified the Supplementary Agreement on the condition that any such agreement would be made by the United States "only in conformity with provisions of statute."[28]

In May 1973, a totalization agreement between the United States and Italy was signed by both countries. Later that year, an attempt was made to enact legislation providing the statutory authority for totalization agreements as required by the Senate in 1953. In November 1973, the Senate approved H.R. 3153 (93rd Congress), a Social Security bill passed by the House in April 1973, adding a provision authorizing the President to enter into totalization agreements with foreign countries and specifying other terms related to such agreements.[29] The version of the bill approved by the House of Representatives did not include a provision relating to totalization agreements. A conference to resolve differences between the House- and Senate-approved versions of the bill was never held and the legislation was not enacted.[30]

The provision in H.R. 3153 (93rd Congress) relating to totalization agreements added by the Senate in 1973 was similar to current law (Section 233 of the Social Security Act), with some notable differences. For example, it provided for a longer period of congressional review. The Senate provision specified that "such an agreement shall become effective on any date provided in the agreement following 90 calendar days of continuous session of the Congress after the date on which the agreement is transmitted ... "[31] In addition, the Senate provision did not specify what action by Congress would be required to stop an agreement from taking effect.

In 1976, the House Ways and Means Committee, Subcommittee on Social Security, held a hearing on the International Social Security Agreements Act (H.R. 14429, 94th Congress), which reflected a proposal supported by the Administration. In contrast to the provision added by the Senate to H.R. 3153 in 1973, H.R. 14429 would have required only that Congress be notified of an international Social Security agreement. Under H.R. 14429, Social Security agreements, like other types of international agreements, would have been reported to Congress *after* (rather than before) entering into force. During the hearing on H.R. 14429, the discussion turned to an alternative "report and wait" provision similar to the one added by the Senate to H.R. 3153 in 1973.[32] The Commissioner of Social Security, James B. Cardwell, indicated that the agency had been advised that the Administration would not object to an arrangement in which Congress would be presented with a proposed Social Security agreement and would have 60 days in which to advise the Administration of their position or otherwise the agreement would become effective. Upon questioning by members of the Social Security Subcommittee, Commissioner Cardwell stated that the agency did not have details on how the process would work. However, the Commissioner indicated that it was his opinion that any objection to an agreement would have to come from Congress, and not from a subcommittee or committee or even one House. [33] Commissioner Cardwell offered to seek clarification on the Administration's position with respect to an appropriate process for congressional review of Social Security agreements.

In a follow-up letter to Honorable James Burke, the Chairman of the Social Security Subcommittee, Commissioner Cardwell expressed the Administration's support for a provision similar to the one added by the Senate to H.R. 3153 in 1973, except with a shorter period of congressional review. The Commissioner stated that the Administration would not object to an arrangement in which a negotiated totalization agreement could not become effective until after 60 days of continuous session of Congress following transmittal to Congress by the President. Under the Administration's provision, if Congress approved of a proposed agreement, no action by Congress would be needed and the agreement would take effect at the end of the specified review period. If Congress disapproved of a proposed agreement, or wanted to alter any of its provisions, Congress would be required to enact a statute to that effect.[34]

In 1977, the statutory authority relating to totalization agreements (Section 233 of the Social Security Act) was established under the Social Security Amendments of 1977 (P.L. 95-216). The provision enacted in 1977 was similar to current law, with some notable differences. For example, under a totalization agreement, an individual may qualify for a benefit from both the United States and the foreign country party to the agreement. The 1977 law specified that, with respect to persons who qualify for benefits under both countries' systems, a totalization agreement could provide that the United States would supplement the total benefit amount (U.S. and foreign benefit combined) payable to a U.S. resident[35] to increase it to the amount he or she would have qualified for under the U.S. system based on the minimum Primary Insurance Amount (PIA) available under current law at the time.[36] In addition, the 1977 law provided for a longer period of congressional review than that supported by the Administration. Specifically, it provided that an agreement would go into effect unless the House of Representatives or the Senate adopted a resolution of disapproval within the period following transmittal to Congress "during which each House of the Congress has been in session on each of 90 days."[37]

The House of Representatives and the Senate initially approved different provisions relating to totalization agreements in considering the 1977 legislation. The provision approved by the House of Representatives specified that each agreement would have to be transmitted to Congress and could not go into effect until after *at least one* House of Congress has been in session for 90 days. During that period, an agreement could be rejected by action of *both* Houses of Congress enacting legislation. The provision approved by the Senate specified that (1) each agreement must be transmitted to Congress with a report on the estimated cost and number of individuals affected; (2) an agreement must not be inconsistent with the provisions of Title II of the Social Security Act; and (3) an agreement could not go into effect until after *each* House of Congress has been in session for 90 days, during which period an agreement could be rejected by action of *either* House of Congress. The conference agreement followed the Senate provision.[38]

In 1981, the Omnibus Budget Reconciliation Act of 1981 (P.L. 97-35) struck the provision in Section 233 of the Social Security Act permitting an agreement to provide that the United States would supplement a U.S. resident's total benefit amount (U.S. and foreign benefit combined) under an agreement if the total benefit amount was less than the minimum benefit he or she would have qualified for under the U.S. system.[39] This was a conforming amendment related to the elimination of the minimum benefit provision under the same law (P.L. 97-35).[40] Accordingly, there is no current law providing for any such supplemental benefit under an agreement.

In 1983, the period for congressional review of Social Security agreements was shortened under the Social Security Amendments of 1983 (P.L. 98-21). The period of congressional review was changed from the period "during which *each* House of the Congress has been in session on each of *90 days*" to the period "during which *at least one* House of the Congress has been in session on each of *60 days*."[41] This is the same period of congressional review provided under current law.[42]

Selection of Partner Countries

The Government Accountability Office (GAO), in a study conducted in 2005, found that the countries with which the United States has entered into Social Security agreements have been selected without a formal guideline or protocol.[43] SSA officials have stated that the agency has used the same major criteria for selecting partner countries since 1978. According to SSA officials, the major criteria used in selecting agreement countries include (1) whether the other country has a Social Security system of general application that pays periodic benefits on account of death, old age or disability; (2) costs to the trust funds; (3) the number of and cost savings to U.S. employers and workers who would benefit from the elimination of dual taxes; (4) the interest of the other country in negotiating an agreement; (5) the ability of the other country to administer an agreement; and (6) input from other U.S. government agencies such as the Department of State and the Office of the U.S. Trade Representative.[44]

In addition, the 2005 GAO Report indicated that SSA is working on initiatives aimed at determining which countries would be suitable partners for future agreements, taking into account the reliability of a country's data and records. According to SSA officials, the agency has sought input from the Department of State and the Department of Commerce working toward developing a more formalized process for identifying potential agreement countries. GAO also reported that SSA has developed a matrix based on 14 economic and administrative factors that may affect a country's ability to determine an individual's eligibility for benefits under an agreement. The purpose of the matrix is to facilitate comparisons among potential agreement countries and evaluate a country's suitability for a future agreement. The matrix also includes factors that could be used to assess the potential impact of an agreement on the Social Security trust funds.[45]

With respect to SSA's initiatives aimed at determining which countries would be suitable partners for future agreements, SSA noted in October 2009:

> Since 2005, SSA has made significant progress toward formalizing its processes for identifying agreement partner countries and evaluating the reliability of a foreign country's data. These advancements include: (1) developing a standardized questionnaire to elicit information on internal controls and information security policies and procedures in force in a potential partner country to protect the integrity of earnings information and the computer network that stores such information; (2) requiring the completion of the questionnaire and a thorough and successful review by SSA experts in order to enter into formal negotiations on a potential totalization agreement; and (3) expanding the actuarial estimates of potential agreements' impact on the U.S. Social Security Trust Funds from short-range, 5-year estimates of the effect to include both short-range (7 year) and long-range (75 year) estimates.[46]

Negotiation and Conclusion of Agreements

Although there are no statutes or regulations regarding the *selection* of potential agreement countries, SSA noted that the agency "has for more than 30 years consistently applied the compatible system, costs/benefits, taxation, practicality and consultative criteria described above in considering possible agreement partner countries."[47] In addition, the negotiation and conclusion of international agreements by SSA are governed by the "Circular 175 Procedure." The Circular 175 Procedure refers to regulations developed by the U.S. Department of State to ensure that treaties and other international agreements are carried out within constitutional and other legal limitations, with due consideration of foreign policy implications, and with appropriate involvement of the State Department.[48] The U.S. Department of State Foreign Affairs Manual states that "[n]egotiations of treaties, or other 'significant' international agreements, or for their extension or revision, are not to be undertaken, nor any exploratory discussions undertaken with representatives of another government or international organization, until authorized in writing by the Secretary or an officer specifically authorized by the Secretary for that purpose."[49]

After authorization is granted by the State Department, SSA officials may negotiate, but not conclude, a Social Security agreement with a foreign country. When negotiations have been completed, SSA's General Counsel reviews the agreement to ensure that it is consistent with U.S. law. In addition, the State Department reviews the agreement to ensure that it conforms to U.S. policy priorities and treaty protocols and that any translation of the agreement is the same in both languages. Following that process, the agreement is signed by an authorized U.S. representative and an authorized representative of the foreign country. After the agreement has been signed, SSA and the foreign Social Security agency meet and address implementation issues, formulating operations procedures to be used in administering the agreement. When that process has been completed, the agreement is forwarded to the U.S. Secretary of State for review. After review at the State Department has been completed, the agreement is sent to the President for review. Finally, the President is required by law to transmit the agreement to Congress for a period of review (60 session days) before the agreement can go into effect.[50] Upon transmittal to Congress, the agreement must be accompanied by a report showing the estimated number of people who will be affected by the agreement and the estimated financial impact of the agreement on programs established by the Social Security Act.[51]

Congressional Review of Agreements

After a Social Security agreement has been entered into with a foreign country, the President is required to transmit the agreement to Congress for a period of review before it can be implemented. [52] There are no rules limiting the amount of time that may elapse between the signing of an agreement and its transmittal to Congress.[53] Although most of the current agreements were transmitted to Congress less than one year after they were signed, there has been some variation. For example, the agreement with Denmark was signed in June 2007 and transmitted to Congress less than a year later in February 2008. The agreement with Canada, which had an additional protocol for Québec, was signed in March 1981 and transmitted to Congress almost three years later in January 1984. The pending agreement with Mexico was signed in June 2004 and has not been transmitted to Congress to date.[54]

Section 233(e)(2) of the Social Security Act specifies that a Social Security agreement automatically goes into effect unless the House of Representatives or the Senate adopts a resolution of disapproval within 60 session days of the agreement's transmittal to Congress.

It should be noted that Section 233(e)(2), which allows for the rejection of a totalization agreement upon adoption of a resolution of disapproval by either House of Congress is functionally identical to the legislative veto provision that was held unconstitutional in *INS v. Chadha*.[55] In that case, the Supreme Court struck down a provision in the Immigration and Nationality Act that gave either House of Congress the authority to overrule deportation decisions made by the Attorney General.[56] The Court declared that a legislative veto constitutes an exercise of legislative power, as its use has "the purpose and effect of altering the legal rights, duties, and relations of persons ... outside the legislative branch."[57] Accordingly, the Court invalidated the disapproval mechanism, holding that Congress may exercise its legislative authority only "in accord with a single, finely wrought and exhaustively considered procedure," namely bicameral passage and presentation to the President.[58] In its decision, the Court explicitly acknowledged that its holding was not limited to the provision at issue, but would instead affect other similar laws, stating: "our inquiry is sharpened rather than blunted by the fact that Congressional veto provisions are appearing with increasing frequency in statutes which delegate authority to executive and independent agencies."[59] The Court has emphasized its categorical disapproval of the legislative veto in subsequent cases, noting in *Printz v. United States*, for instance, that "the legislative veto, though enshrined in perhaps hundreds of federal statutes ... was nonetheless held unconstitutional" in *Chadha*.[60] The maxim delineated in *Chadha*, as consistently reaffirmed by the Court, is fully applicable in the current context.[61] Accordingly, given that the disapproval mechanism in Section 233(e)(2) authorizes "congressional invalidation of executive action" outside the strictures of bicameralism and presentment, there is no discernible basis upon which it may be argued successfully that its utilization by Congress would withstand judicial scrutiny.[62]

Congress has never rejected a Social Security agreement. As a result, the apparent constitutional infirmity of Section 233(e)(2) has not been an issue. Congressional utilization of the mechanism in Section 233(e)(2) to reject a Social Security agreement could give rise to a judicial challenge, potentially resulting in an invalidation of the disapproval mechanism and a determination that the agreement is effective. Specifically, in considering the effect of the unconstitutional disapproval mechanism, a reviewing court would consider whether the remainder of Section 233 is valid, or whether the entire statute must be nullified. The Supreme Court has held that "[u]nless it is evident that the Legislature would not have enacted those provisions which are within its power, independently of that which is not, the invalid part may be dropped if what is left is a fully operative law."[63] In *Westcott v. Califano*, the court noted that "the existence of a broad severability clause in the Social Security Act reflects the Congressional wish that judicial interpretation of the act leave as much of the statute intact as possible."[64] The existence of this severability clause, coupled with the fact that the operative provisions of Section 233 would remain fully functional absent the disapproval mechanism in Subsection (e)(2), gives rise to the likelihood that a reviewing court would invalidate any attempt to utilize the disapproval mechanism, while giving effect to an otherwise properly executed Social Security agreement.[65]

Before the 1983 Supreme Court Decision of *INS v. Chadha*, other acts had provisions similar to the legislative veto provision found in Section 233(e)(2) of the Social Security Act. In response to the Court's holding in *Chadha*, legislative veto provisions in other Acts were replaced with provisions requiring Congress to adopt a joint resolution of approval or disapproval. For example, the Fishery Conservation and Management Act of 1976, as amended, specified that international fisheries agreements would enter into force after a 60-day waiting period unless Congress adopts a joint resolution of disapproval.[66]

Implementation of Agreements

It is the responsibility of the Social Security Administration to make rules and regulations and to establish procedures necessary to implement and administer international Social Security agreements.[67] Each agreement is accompanied by an *Administrative Arrangement for the Implementation of the Agreement on Social Security* that may be signed when the agreement is signed or at a later time. The administrative arrangement provides general guidelines for the implementation and administration of the agreement, as well as specific rules regarding cooperation between partner countries. For example, it requires the exchange of statistics on the number of beneficiaries and the total amount of benefits paid. It also provides for the exchange of information needed to adjudicate claims filed under the agreement.[68]

Changes and Termination of Agreements

International Social Security agreements and their administrative protocols can be amended. The agreements require that the parties involved communicate to each other any changes in their laws that could affect the application of an agreement. When changes are made to a country's Social Security system that affect the application of an agreement, a supplementary agreement (which updates and amends the original agreement) must be signed. For example, the United States and Sweden signed a supplementary agreement in 2004 to take into account a major reform of Sweden's Social Security system in which the defined benefit public pension system was replaced with a new system that includes mandatory individual accounts, among other features. The supplementary agreement updated and clarified several provisions of the original agreement to reflect other changes in U.S. and Swedish laws since the original agreement was signed in 1985.

Social Security agreements can be terminated by one of the countries party to the agreement. If an agreement is terminated, it typically remains in effect for a 12-month period following the month in which notification is given by one of the parties. Benefits in payment at the time of termination would be retained. Individuals whose claims are in process, or those who would become entitled to benefits before the end of the 12-month period, would retain entitlement to benefits under the agreement. No agreements have been terminated to date.

CURRENT SOCIAL SECURITY AGREEMENTS

The United States has Social Security agreements in force with 24 countries (see **Table 2**). In addition, the United States has a pending agreement with Mexico that was signed on June 29, 2004. As noted previously, the agreement with Mexico has not been transmitted to Congress. Reportedly, as of January 2010, the agreement remains under review at SSA (SSA has not forwarded the agreement to the State Department).[69]

Although the specific terms of each Social Security agreement may differ given the variation in Social Security systems in each country, the provisions of an agreement must be consistent with the Social Security Act. Section 233(c)(4) of the Social Security Act states "any such agreement may contain other provisions which are not inconsistent with the other provisions of [Title II of the Social Security Act] and which the President deems appropriate to carry out the purposes of this section." A description and the complete text of each agreement are available on the Social Security Administration's website.[70] In December 2007, about $28 million was paid in monthly benefits to about 146,200 recipients under U.S. Social Security agreements (see **Table 3**).[71]

Table 2. U.S. Social Security Agreements in Force

Country	Effective Date
Australia	October 1, 2002
Austria	November 1, 1991
Belgium	July 1, 1984
Canada	August 1, 1984
Chile	December 1, 2001
Czech Republic	January 1, 2009
Denmark	October 1, 2008
Finland	November 1, 1992
France	July 1, 1988
Germany	December 1, 1979
Greece	September 1, 1994
Ireland	September 1, 1993
Italy	November 1, 1978
Japan	October 1, 2005
Korea, South	April 1, 2001

Table 2. (Continued)

Country	Effective Date
Luxembourg	November 1, 1993
Netherlands	November 1, 1990
Norway	July 1, 1984
Poland	March 1, 2009
Portugal	August 1, 1989
Spain	April 1, 1988
Sweden	January 1, 1987
Switzerland	November 1, 1980
United Kingdom	1985/1988a

Source: Social Security Administration, Status of Totalization Agreements, available at http://www.ssa.gov/ international/status.html.

Note: The agreements with Austria, Belgium, Germany, Sweden and Switzerland permit an individual to receive benefits as a dependent or survivor of a worker while a *resident* in those countries only if the worker is a U.S. citizen or a citizen of the country of residence.

a. Provisions that eliminate double taxation became effective January 1, 1985; provisions that allow persons to use work in both countries to qualify for benefits became effective January 1, 1988.

Totalization Benefits

Benefit Application Process

Individuals living in the United States may apply for totalization benefits[72] at any one of the approximately 1,300 SSA field offices in the United States.[73] Individuals living outside the United States generally are required to apply for totalization benefits at a Foreign Service Post (FSP) located in a U.S. embassy or consulate, or at the social security agency in their home country.[74]

Initial processing of applications for totalization benefits is handled by SSA field office staff or Foreign Service Nationals in the FSP. Among other tasks, these individuals are responsible for reviewing supporting documents, such as birth and marriage certificates. After initial processing, application packages are sent to SSA's Office of International Operations (OIO), which is responsible for final adjudication of claims for U.S. totalization benefits.[75] For claims filed at an SSA field office (rather than a FSP), OIO requests the foreign coverage record from the foreign social security agency.[76] OIO reviews the supporting documents (such as evidence of identity and citizenship), develops additional evidence if needed, and makes a final decision on the claim.[77] If the claim is for U.S. totalization disability benefits, OIO will make the determination of disability, however, Disability Determination Services may be asked to develop the medical evidence in such cases.[78]

Table 3. Number of Beneficiaries and Average Monthly Benefit Under U.S. Social Security Agreements, December 2007

Country	Total	Retired Workers	Disabled Workers	Wives and Husbands	Widow(er)s[a]	Children
	Number of Beneficiaries					
Overall	**146,199**	**96,970**	**2,752**	**32,484**	**12,525**	**1,468**
Australia	1,201	866	90	208	20	17
Austria	1,249	919	53	191	54	32
Belgium	752	517	6	147	68	14
Canada	47,193	29,876	1,274	9,725	5,859	459
Chile	98	77	b	17	b	b
Finland	271	187	16	52	11	5
France	4,498	3,206	24	824	371	73
Germany	19,926	14,785	521	3,228	1,168	224
Greece	3,371	2,311	147	598	260	55
Ireland	1,846	1,296	25	376	120	29
Italy	9,075	5,792	102	1,770	1,293	118
Japan	22,520	13,012	b	8,669	773	b
Korea, S.	432	307	b	119	6	b
Luxembourg	58	35	7	10	b	b
Netherlands	2,676	1,878	6	587	177	28
Norway	3,907	2,546	76	816	432	37
Portugal	2,009	1,308	111	318	238	34
Spain	2,531	1,592	72	516	299	52
Sweden	2,197	1,623	29	422	94	29
Switzerland	4,168	3,006	43	842	229	48
U.K.	16,221	11,831	149	3,049	1,046	146
	Average Monthly Benefit (U.S. dollars)					
Overall	**$193.20**	**Overall**	**$193.20**	**Overall**	**$193.20**	**Overall**

Table 3. (Continued)

Country	Total	Retired Workers	Disabled Workers	Wives and Husbands	Widow(er)s[a]	Children
Australia	207.73	214.39	444.33	85.57	242.30	69.35
Austria	208.22	237.64	293.88	70.93	165.14	113.50
Belgium	192.58	226.05	543.50	77.86	174.11	100.57
Canada	169.04	196.56	396.18	71.87	145.03	112.61
Chile	202.10	221.85	b	88.94	b	b
Finland	196.69	207.10	493.69	79.53	170.45	133.00
France	207.32	243.50	489.98	81.61	175.78	104.51
Germany	223.65	253.74	455.77	73.56	175.04	114.62
Greece	174.63	188.08	413.53	74.71	164.33	105.95
Ireland	209.35	239.50	647.46	83.60	210.29	110.69
Italy	180.43	214.49	529.47	74.37	151.86	110.70
Japan	193.70	246.41	b	110.12	247.16	b
Korea, S.	203.54	239.11	b	110.60	226.57	b
Luxembourg	255.12	270.69	441.86	81.50	b	b
Netherlands	186.80	218.39	965.83	79.26	189.81	136.43
Norway	186.70	211.61	432.33	81.97	198.78	137.49
Portugal	194.07	203.04	486.24	75.91	174.75	135.74
Spain	174.56	200.47	426.10	73.09	160.79	119.25
Sweden	170.95	190.68	412.72	77.92	184.76	133.83
Switzerland	181.61	209.16	463.21	75.55	174.70	96.96
U.K.	239.19	281.83	510.31	83.40	190.29	110.92

Source: SSA, Social Security Bulletin, Annual Statistical Supplement, 2008, Table 5.M 1, available at https://www.socialsecurity.gov/policy/docs/statcomps/supplement/2008/5m.pdf.

Note: Three countries with which the United States has an agreement are not shown in this table (Czech Republic, Denmark and Poland) because these agreements went into effect after 2007.

a. Number includes nondisabled and disabled widow(er)s, mothers and fathers, and parents. A mother's/father's benefit is a monthly benefit payable to a widow/widower or surviving divorced mother/father if (1) the deceased worker on whose account the benefit is paid was either fully or currently insured at the time of death and (2) an entitled child of the worker in her/his care is under age 16 or is disabled. A parent's benefit is a monthly benefit payable to a dependent parent aged 62 or older of a deceased fully insured worker.

b. Number not shown to avoid disclosure of information regarding particular individuals.

Although agreements allow for some variation in the application process for totalization benefits,[79] each of the offices involved in the process (SSA field offices, SSA's Office of International Operations, and FSPs) maintain certain responsibilities. For individuals applying in the United States, SSA field offices are responsible for taking claims for U.S. totalization benefits, as well as claims for regular or totalization benefits from foreign countries. OIO is responsible for liaison activities with foreign countries, which include requesting foreign coverage records and providing U.S. coverage records or other information to foreign countries. In addition, OIO is responsible for final adjudication of a claim for U.S. totalization benefits. For individuals applying outside the United States, the FSPs, like the SSA field offices, are responsible for the development of benefit claims. The specific procedures vary depending on the terms of each agreement and whether the claim is filed initially at the FSP or the foreign social security agency. [80]

Computation of Benefits

Workers who meet the minimum coverage requirement for a U.S. Social Security benefit based on combined U.S. and foreign work credits can receive a totalization benefit (assuming all other eligibility requirements are met). A totalization benefit is prorated to reflect the number of years the worker was covered by the U.S. system.

For *regular* (non-totalization) benefits, the worker's Primary Insurance Amount (PIA)[81] is computed by applying the Social Security benefit formula to the worker's Average Indexed Monthly Earnings (AIME). The AIME is computed by dividing the worker's 35 highest years of covered earnings, adjusted for the growth in average wages over time, by the computation period (35 years or 420 months). If a worker has fewer than 35 years of covered earnings, years of zero earnings are counted in the computation of the AIME, resulting in a lower initial monthly benefit amount. For workers who reach the age of 62, become disabled, or die in 2010, the benefit formula that is applied to the worker's AIME to compute his or her PIA is:

90% of the first $761 of AIME, *plus*

32% of AIME over $761 through $4,586, *plus*

15% of AIME over $4,586.[82]

As with regular benefits, the amount of a U.S. totalization benefit depends on the duration of the worker's coverage under the U.S. system and his or her level of earnings. The process for computing a totalization benefit, however, differs from the regular benefit computation process according to the following basic steps:

> (1) a theoretical full-career earnings record is created based on the worker's actual earnings under the U.S. system relative to the average earnings of all covered workers;
>
> (2) a theoretical PIA is computed based on the theoretical earnings record;
>
> (3) the theoretical PIA is multiplied by a pro rata fraction to determine the pro rata PIA;[83] and
>
> (4) the monthly benefit amount is established based on the pro rata PIA (i.e., any adjustments that apply, such as a reduction for early retirement, are made to the pro rata PIA to determine the monthly benefit amount).[84]

Stated simply, a theoretical benefit is computed as though the individual had worked a full career (a coverage lifetime)[85] under the U.S. system at the same level of earnings he or she had during actual periods of covered employment in the United States. The theoretical benefit is prorated to reflect the proportion of the worker's coverage lifetime completed under the U.S. system.

By definition, totalization beneficiaries have fewer than 40 quarters (10 years) of Social Security- covered employment in the United States.[86] Because totalization benefits are prorated to reflect the worker's period of coverage under the U.S. system, totalization benefits on average are lower than regular benefits. For example, in December 2007, the average monthly benefit under U.S. totalization agreements for retired workers was $227.54 (see **Table 3**). Among regular beneficiaries, the average monthly benefit for retired workers was $1,079.[87]

Based on combined (totalized) work credits, a worker may qualify for Social Security benefits under one or both country's systems, depending on the eligibility requirements in each country. Totalization benefits are paid independently by each country (i.e., a U.S. Social Security benefit payable under a totalization agreement is paid separately from a benefit payable under a foreign system).[88] In addition, a U.S. totalization benefit may be converted to a regular benefit if the beneficiary continues to work in Social Security-covered employment in the United States and obtains enough work credits to become fully insured under the U.S. system without taking into account foreign work credits.[89]

Monitoring of Beneficiaries

The Social Security Administration monitors the continuing eligibility of Social Security beneficiaries (totalized and regular beneficiaries) living in the United States and abroad. With respect to beneficiaries living in the United States, SSA relies on data matching with states and federal agencies to identify circumstances that could affect an individual's continuing eligibility for benefits or the proper benefit amount (such as changes in work activity) and unreported deaths. With respect to beneficiaries living outside the United States (U.S. citizens and noncitizens), SSA relies on personal questionnaires (Foreign Enforcement Questionnaires) and periodic validation surveys (i.e., visits to beneficiaries' homes) to verify an individual's continuing eligibility for benefits.

SSA mails Foreign Enforcement Questionnaires (FEQs) to beneficiaries who live outside the United States on an annual or biennial basis, depending on factors such as the beneficiary's country of residence, age, and whether he or she has a representative payee.[90] For example, beneficiaries with a representative payee and those who are aged 97 or older are sent a questionnaire each year. Generally, beneficiaries who receive their own benefits (i.e., those who do not have a representative payee) are sent a questionnaire every other year, unless they live in certain countries to which questionnaires are sent annually.[91] The completed questionnaire must be returned to SSA within 60 days. The questionnaires are intended to provide SSA with information needed to verify the individual's continuing eligibility for benefits and the proper benefit amount (for example, an individual's benefit payments could be affected by changes in work activity or marital status as well as improvement of a disabling condition). The 2005 GAO Report indicated that SSA relies on foreign beneficiaries to accurately *self-report* the information because the agency does not conduct independent verification of the responses. Among other reasons, GAO indicated that SSA does not have the capability to verify information for foreign beneficiaries using computer database matches (as it does for domestic beneficiaries) and is unable to independently verify the death of foreign beneficiaries. GAO also pointed out, however, that SSA is developing pilot computer match projects with Italy and Germany to establish an independent, third-party mechanism for verifying beneficiaries' continuing eligibility for benefits.[92]

With respect to SSA's computer match projects, SSA noted in October 2009 that since 2005:

> SSA has initiated data matching projects under current totalization agreements to support and expand its stewardship initiatives. SSA has begun automated death data exchanges with a number of totalization partner countries designed to identify deceased beneficiaries and avoid overpayment of benefits. Some of the results of these efforts are as follows:
>
> A one-way death data exchange with Germany resulted in overpayment savings of $1,792,546 (U.S. dollars).
>
> Since February 2009, SSA has implemented recurring death data exchanges with Australia. These data exchanges have resulted in overpayment savings of $128,878.70 (U.S. dollars).
>
> In 2009, SSA is working to expand the death data exchange to five additional totalization partner countries.
>
> SSA will pilot two additional automated death data exchanges before the end of 2009.
>
> SSA intends to conduct automated death data exchanges with all totalization agreement partner countries.[93]

In addition, SSA conducts periodic validation surveys in foreign countries (including countries with which the United States has totalization agreements) where Social Security beneficiaries live. SSA staff (from the Office of Central Operations) and foreign service staff visit beneficiaries' homes to administer the surveys for the purpose of verifying the identity and continuing eligibility of beneficiaries. SSA conducts validation surveys in about three countries each year. The frequency of visits varies by country, depending on factors such as results of past surveys and evidence of data reliability concerns. For example, some countries may be surveyed every five years (such as Portugal) while others may be surveyed every 30 years (such as Sweden). Although validation surveys have helped SSA identify unreported deaths and overpayments, the 2005 GAO Report indicated that, according to SSA officials, the validation surveys conducted since 2000 generally verify only the identity and existence of beneficiaries.

They do not verify work activity or other information that could affect an individual's benefit payments.[94]

Effects of Agreements on Selected Provisions of the Social Security Act

Waiver of the Alien Nonpayment Provision

Section 202(y) of the Social Security Act requires noncitizens in the United States to be lawfully present to receive benefits.[95] If a noncitizen is entitled to benefits, but does not meet the lawful presence requirement, his or her benefits are suspended. In such cases, a noncitizen may receive benefits (which may include benefits based on work performed in the United States without authorization)[96] while residing outside the United States if he or she meets one of the exceptions to the alien nonpayment provision under Section 202(t) of the Social Security Act (see **Table 4**). Under the alien nonpayment provision, a noncitizen's benefits are suspended if he or she remains outside the United States[97] for more than six consecutive months,[98] unless one of several broad exceptions is met.[99] For example, an alien may receive benefits outside the United States if he or she is a citizen of a country that has a social insurance or pension system that pays benefits to eligible U.S. citizens residing outside that country[100] (see **Appendix B**), or if he or she is a resident of a country with which the United States has a totalization agreement (see **Table 2**). If an alien does not meet one of the exceptions to the alien nonpayment provision, his or her benefits are suspended beginning with the seventh month of absence and are not resumed until he or she returns to the United States lawfully for a full calendar month.

In addition, to receive payments outside the United States, alien *dependents and survivors* must have lived in the United States previously for at least five years (lawfully or unlawfully), and the family relationship to the worker must have existed during that time (see Table 5). The law provides several broad exceptions to the five-year U.S. residency requirement for alien dependents and survivors (see Table 6). For example, an alien dependent or survivor is exempt from the U.S. residency requirement if he or she is a citizen of a treaty obligation country (i.e., if nonpayment of benefits would be contrary to a treaty between the United States and the individual's country of citizenship; see Appendix B), or if he or she is a citizen or resident of a country with which the United States has a totalization agreement (see Table 2).

Tables 4 through 6 summarize the complex rules and exceptions that apply to the payment of benefits to noncitizens living outside the United States (payments to workers and their family members). As shown in the tables, assuming all other eligibility requirements are met, the existence of a totalization agreement between the United States and a foreign country (1) allows workers and their family members who are residents of the foreign country to receive benefits outside the United States indefinitely (i.e., the alien nonpayment provision is waived)[101] and (2) may allow family members (dependents and survivors of the worker) who are citizens or residents of the foreign country to receive benefits outside the United States without having to meet the U.S. residency requirement (i.e., the five-year U.S. residency requirement that applies to alien dependents and survivors outside the United States is waived).[102]

These advantages of a totalization agreement are not limited to workers (and their family members) who qualify for U.S. Social Security benefits based on work performed in the United States under a formal arrangement between the United States and a foreign country under the terms of a totalization agreement. Workers (and their family members) who qualify for U.S. Social Security benefits (which may include benefits based on work performed in the United States without authorization) would be exempt from the payment restrictions that apply to noncitizens residing outside the United States (including the five-year U.S. residency requirement for dependents and survivors). This means that, depending on the specific agreement and on whether SSA has determined that the other country reciprocates under the provisions of Section 202(t) of the Social Security Act, dependents and survivors of noncitizen workers who reside outside the United States and who may never have resided in the United States could collect U.S. Social Security benefits on the worker's record. In addition, citizens of third-party countries (countries other than the United States or a totalization agreement country) are exempt from these payment restrictions (including the five-year U.S. residency requirement for dependents and survivors) if they *reside* in a country with which the United States has a totalization agreement.

In addition to the alien nonpayment provision, other restrictions apply to the payment of benefits to individuals residing outside the United States. U.S. Treasury Department regulations and Social Security restrictions prohibit payments from being sent to individuals residing in Cuba, North Korea, Cambodia, Vietnam, or areas that were in the former Soviet Union (excluding Armenia, Estonia, Latvia, Lithuania and Russia); in countries with Social Security restrictions in place, exceptions to the general nonpayment rule can be made for certain eligible beneficiaries.[103]

Table 4. Exceptions to the Alien Nonpayment Provision for Workers and Dependents/Survivors

An alien's benefits are suspended if he or she is outside the United States for more than six consecutive months, unless one of the following exceptions is met:
• the individual is a citizen of a country that has a social insurance or pension system under which benefits are paid to eligible U.S. citizens who reside outside that country (see Appendix B for a list of countries)
• the individual is entitled to benefits on the earnings record of a worker who lived in the United States for at least 10 years or earned at least 40 quarters of coverage under the U.S. Social Security system
• the individual is entitled to benefits on the earnings record of a worker who had railroad employment covered by Social Security
• the individual is outside the United States while in the active military or naval service of the United States
• the individual is entitled to benefits on the earnings record of a worker who died while in the U.S. military service or as a result of a service-connected disease or injury
• the nonpayment of benefits would be contrary to a treaty obligation of the United States in effect as of August 1, 1956 (i.e., the individual is a citizen of a treaty obligation country; see Appendix B for a list of countries)
• the individual is a resident of a country with which the United States has a totalization agreementa (see Table 2 for a list of countries)
• the individual was eligible for Social Security benefits as of December 1956

Source: Section 202(t) of the Social Security Act.

a. Under the agreement with Australia, the United States pays Social Security benefits to an Australian citizen who resides in the United States, Australia, or a third country with which the United States has a totalization agreement. If an Australian citizen resides elsewhere, he or she is subject to the alien nonpayment provision. The agreement with Denmark contains a similar provision.

The Social Security Act also prohibits the payment of benefits to most individuals who are removed from the United States (i.e., deported).[104]

Legislative History of Payment Rules for Noncitizens

When the Social Security program began paying benefits in 1940, there were no restrictions on benefit payments to noncitizens. In 1956, amid concerns that noncitizens were working in the United States for relatively short periods and returning to their native countries where they and their family members would collect benefits for many years, Congress enacted restrictions on benefits for alien *workers* living abroad (restrictions did not apply to alien dependents and survivors). The Social Security Amendments of 1956 (P.L. 84-880) required noncitizens to reside in the United States to receive benefits and, under the alien nonpayment provision, suspended benefits if the recipient remained outside the United States for more than six consecutive months, with broad exceptions (see Table 4).

In 1983, Congress placed restrictions on benefit payments to alien *dependents and survivors* living abroad. The Social Security Amendments of 1983 (P.L. 98-21) made alien dependents and survivors outside the United States subject to the same payment restrictions as alien workers. P.L. 98-2 1 further required that, to receive benefits outside the United States, alien dependents and survivors (or their parents, in the case of a child's benefit) must have lived in the United States previously for at least five years (see Table 5), with broad exceptions (see Table 6).

Table 5. Additional Residency Requirement for Alien Dependents and Survivors Outside the United States

In addition to the requirements shown in **Table 4**, to receive payments outside the United States, an alien dependent or survivor must have lived in the United States for at least five years (lawfully or unlawfully) under one of the following circumstances:
A spouse, divorced spouse, widow(er), surviving divorced spouse, or surviving divorced mother or father:
must have resided in the United States for at least five years and the spousal relationship to the worker must have existed during that time
A child:
must have resided in the United States for at least five years as the child of the worker; or the worker and the child's other parent (if any) each must have either resided in the United States for at least five years or died while residing in the United States
An adopted child:
must have been adopted in the United States; *and* lived in the United States with the worker; *and* received at least half of his or her support from the worker in the year before the worker's entitlement or death

Source: Section 202(t) of the Social Security Act.

Note: The five-year period of residence in the United States does not have to be continuous (20 C.F.R. § 404.460).

Table 6. Exceptions to the Additional Residency Requirement for Alien Dependents and Survivors Outside the United States

An alien dependent or survivor living outside the United States is not subject to the five-year U.S. residency requirement if one of the following exceptions is met:
• the individual was eligible for Social Security benefits before January 1, 1985
• the individual is entitled to benefits on the earnings record of a worker who died while in the U.S. military service or as a result of a service-connected disease or injury
• the nonpayment of benefits would be contrary to a treaty obligation of the United States in effect as of August 1, 1956 (i.e., the individual is a citizen of a treaty obligation country; see Appendix B for a list of countries)
• the individual is a citizen or resident of a country with which the United States has a totalization agreementa (see Table 2 for a list of countries)

Source: Section 202(t) of the Social Security Act.

a. Under the agreement with Australia, Australian dependents and survivors who do not reside in the United States, Australia, or a third country with which the United States has a totalization agreement must meet the five-year U.S. residency requirement to receive payments abroad. The agreement with Denmark contains a similar provision.

Several factors led to the enactment of tighter restrictions on benefit payments to alien dependents and survivors living abroad in 1983, including the large number of dependents that were being added to the benefit rolls (in some cases under fraudulent circumstances) after workers had returned to their native country and become entitled to benefits, and difficulties associated with monitoring the continuing eligibility of recipients living abroad.

At the time, GAO estimated that, of the 164,000 dependents living abroad in 1981, 56,000 were added to the benefit rolls after the worker became entitled to benefits. Of that number, an estimated 51,000 (or 91%) were noncitizens.[105] Two years earlier, the Commissioner of Social Security stated that SSA investigators had found evidence that some recipients living abroad were faking marriages and adoptions and failing to report deaths in order to "cheat the system." At the time, the Commissioner stated that such problems were particularly acute in Greece, Italy, Mexico and the Philippines where large numbers of beneficiaries were residing. He stated further that, in some countries, "there is a kind of industry built up of so-called claims-fixers who, for a percentage of the benefit, will work to ensure that somebody gets the maximum benefit they can possibly get out of the system."[106]

In 1996, Congress enacted tighter restrictions on the payment of Social Security benefits to aliens residing in the United States. The Personal Responsibility and Work Opportunity Reconciliation Act of 1996 (PRWORA)[107] prohibited the payment of Social Security benefits to aliens in the United States who are not lawfully present, unless nonpayment would be contrary to a totalization agreement or Section 202(t) of the Social Security Act (the alien nonpayment provision). This provision became effective for applications filed on or after September 1, 1996. Subsequently, the Illegal Immigration Reform and Immigrant Responsibility Act of 1996[108] added Section 202(y) to the Social Security Act. Section 202(y) of the Social Security Act, which became effective for applications filed on or after December 1, 1996, states:

> Notwithstanding any other provision of law, no monthly benefit under [Title II of the Social Security Act] shall be payable to any alien in the United States for any month during which such alien is not lawfully present in the United States as determined by the Attorney General.

Exemption from the Windfall Elimination Provision

Generally, under a provision of the Social Security Act known as the windfall elimination provision (WEP), individuals who receive a pension from work that was not covered by the U.S. Social Security system (a noncovered pension) are subject to a reduction in Social Security retirement and disability benefits if they have fewer than 30 years of Social Security coverage.[109] Under the Social Security Independence and Program Improvements Act of 1994 (P.L. 103-296), the WEP does not apply to U.S. *totalization* benefits payable beginning January 1995.[110]

In addition, a foreign pension based on a totalization agreement with the United States does not trigger the WEP in the computation of a *regular* (non-totalization) U.S. benefit for benefits payable beginning January 1995 (i.e., a foreign pension may trigger the WEP only if the worker is insured based on U.S. coverage alone and the foreign pension is not based on a totalization agreement with the United States).[111]

Application of a Work Test

Social Security beneficiaries who continue to work are subject to a limitation on earnings until they reach the full retirement age (FRA).[112] There are two types of work tests: the Retirement Earnings Test and the Foreign Work Test. The Retirement Earnings Test (RET) applies to work performed by beneficiaries in the United States and to work performed by beneficiaries outside the United States if the work is covered by the U.S. Social Security program. Under the RET, Social Security benefits are subject to a withholding of $1 for every $2 of earnings above $14,160 for beneficiaries who are below the FRA and will not reach the FRA in 2010. For beneficiaries who will reach the FRA in 2010, Social Security benefits are subject to a withholding of $1 for every $3 of earnings above $37,680.[113] The Foreign Work Test applies to work performed by beneficiaries outside the United States if the work is not covered by the U.S. Social Security program. Under the Foreign Work Test, Social Security benefits are withheld for each month a beneficiary below the FRA works more than 45 hours outside the United States in a job that is not subject to U.S. Social Security taxes (regardless of the amount of earnings).[114]

The Social Security Act extends U.S. Social Security coverage to U.S. citizens and residents working abroad. However, totalization agreements modify the rules of coverage allowing work performed by U.S. citizens and residents in a foreign country to be covered under either the U.S. system or the foreign system, depending on the terms of the agreement. Therefore, totalization agreements affect whether a Social Security beneficiary working outside the United States is subject to the Retirement Earnings Test or the Foreign Work Test.[115]

Qualification for Medicare Hospital Insurance

Medicare is a federal health insurance program for persons aged 65 or older, under the age of 65 with certain disabilities, and any age with End Stage Renal Disease (ESRD).[116] Social Security beneficiaries are eligible for Medicare at the age of 65. Social Security disability beneficiaries are eligible for Medicare at any age after they have been receiving disability benefits for 24 months. ESRD beneficiaries are eligible if they have permanent kidney failure requiring dialysis or a kidney transplant.[117] Totalization agreements do not extend Medicare coverage to totalization beneficiaries. Specifically, Section 233(c)(3) of the Social Security Act prohibits totalization beneficiaries from entitlement to Medicare premium-free Hospital Insurance (HI) benefits.[118]

However, a person who is entitled to U.S. totalization benefits may qualify for Medicare premium-free HI, but he or she must meet the requirements independently of an agreement.[119] For example, a totalization beneficiary may be entitled to Medicare premium-free HI if he or she is also entitled to regular benefits on a Social Security Number (SSN) that is different from the SSN on which totalization benefits are paid. [120] In addition, a totalization beneficiary may meet the requirements for a regular benefit[121] that is denied or terminated because the regular benefit would be lower than the totalization benefit.[122] In this case, the beneficiary may maintain his or her status as a totalization beneficiary to receive the higher benefit amount and may be entitled to Medicare premium-free HI. A totalization beneficiary who does not meet the requirements for premium-free Medicare HI may be able to get Medicare HI by paying a monthly premium.[123]

Issues and Concerns

Many observers agree that international Social Security agreements can be beneficial for U.S. companies and workers. However, some policymakers have expressed concerns about several aspects of the agreements. Among these concerns are (1) SSA's policies and procedures for assessing the integrity and reliability of foreign data and evidentiary documents to identify potential risks when entering into an agreement; (2) SSA's ability to verify individuals' initial eligibility for benefits under an agreement and to monitor the continuing eligibility of beneficiaries outside the United States; and (3) the role of Congress with respect to the approval process for potential agreements, as well as the need for enhanced reporting requirements and periodic evaluation of agreements once they are in force.[124]

Assessing Risks Associated with Future Agreements

In 2005, GAO reported concerns regarding the potential exposure of the Social Security trust funds to improper payments resulting from inaccurate or falsified foreign data and documentation (such as birth, death, marriage and divorce records). GAO reported that "Historically, SSA has conducted only limited reviews, focusing primarily on broad policy issues and systems compatibility, rather than examining the integrity and reliability of earnings data and evidentiary documents."[125] However, GAO also reported that SSA was in the process of developing new initiatives to identify risks associated with totalization agreements. GAO further stated:

> SSA officials told us that the agency has developed several new initiatives to identify risks associated with totalization agreements. SSA has developed a standardized questionnaire to help the agency identify and assess the reliability of earnings data in countries under consideration for future totalization agreements. In addition, SSA has undertaken two initiatives aimed at determining which countries may be suitable for future agreements. One initiative involves conducting discussions with other U.S. government agencies such as the Department of Commerce to better assess which countries may be suitable for future agreements. SSA is also developing a matrix to compare relevant factors, including data accessibility across countries where agreements could be negotiated in the future. Finally, in an effort to improve existing procedures, SSA is conducting numerous "vulnerability assessments" to detect potential problems with the accuracy of foreign countries' documents.[126]

Despite these initiatives, GAO cautioned in 2005:

> While these tools appear to be a positive first step for helping SSA identify potential risks associated with future totalization agreements, SSA has only recently begun implementing them and has not developed plans to integrate these initiatives into formal procedures. The lack of a formal protocol, coupled with the expected retirement of key management and staff over the next few years, may result in the loss of important institutional knowledge relating to totalization agreements, which may hinder the agency's ability to effectively assess risks associated with future agreements.[127]

Determining Eligibility for Benefits under an Agreement

In 2005, GAO reported concerns regarding SSA's ability (1) to determine individuals' initial eligibility for benefits under an agreement, and (2) to monitor beneficiaries outside the United States with respect to continuing eligibility for benefits once an agreement is in force. GAO reported:

> Our review also identified potential vulnerabilities in SSA's policies and procedures for verifying individuals' eligibility for benefits once an agreement is in force. When establishing an individual's initial eligibility for benefits, the agency generally accepts critical documentation from foreign countries, such as birth certificates, without independently verifying the accuracy of such information. We also found that SSA's two primary tools for determining an individual's continuing eligibility – validation surveys and personal questionnaires – may be insufficient to ensure that only those still eligible for benefits continue to receive them.[128]

In response, SSA pointed out that the process for evaluating foreign evidence in totalization claims is the same as that for regular claims. SSA maintains, therefore, that totalization agreements do not introduce a new element of risk to the Social Security program. [129] SSA further pointed out that detailed procedures and guidelines are used in evaluating foreign evidence, as described in the agency's Program Operations Manual System.[130]

Despite the existing procedures and guidelines, GAO cautioned in 2005:

> Once totalization agreements are in force, verification of individuals' initial and continuing eligibility for benefits is essential to ensure that benefits are paid only to entitled recipients. The relatively limited scope of SSA's current verification procedures may not provide adequate assurance that the trust funds are protected from improper payments. Moreover, because the agency lacks the ability to independently verify the information it receives from foreign beneficiaries on its questionnaires, SSA has little assurance that questionnaire responses are accurate. Thus, SSA may not be aware of changes in beneficiaries' eligibility status, resulting in improper payments for an extended period of time. Given the likely growth in the number of foreign beneficiaries in coming years, including totalized beneficiaries, the trust funds will likely face increased exposure if existing processes are not improved. In an environment of limited staff and budgetary resources, SSA could benefit from a more systematic approach for independently verifying information that can affect individuals' initial and continuing eligibility for benefits, such as computer matches. While SSA has taken some positive steps in this regard such as its negotiations for conducting a death match with Italy, additional challenges remain. In particular, the agency currently lacks the authority to conduct computer matches with foreign countries – a prerequisite for conducting such matches and other forms of independent verification with foreign countries.[131]

Related Testimony by GAO and SSA in 2006

In 2006, GAO raised similar concerns regarding totalization agreements in testimony before the House Ways and Means Committee, Subcommittee on Social Security.[132] A summary table showing the status of recommendations made in the 2005 GAO Report regarding totalization agreements indicates that, while the recommendations had not been implemented at that time, SSA was making progress toward them. For example, it was reported that SSA had developed a standardized questionnaire to assess the reliability of earnings data in countries that may be considered for future totalization agreements. It was also reported that SSA was exploring a more systematic approach, such as the use of computer matches, to independently verify data from foreign countries. A GAO official testified in 2006:

> While SSA is making progress in improving the program's integrity by strengthening its procedures for verifying documents and coordinating with other agencies and foreign governments, opportunities remain for additional progress. SSA plans further enhancements to the Enumeration at Entry program in order to protect against errors, fraud and abuse. In addition, a more systematic approach to verifying data from other countries with which we have totalization agreements can help ensure proper payments of benefits and prompt notice of the death of beneficiaries. SSA will, however, continue to face challenges in its dealings with noncitizens. Changes in immigration laws and shortcomings in the enforcement of those laws make it difficult for SSA to identify noncitizens who are eligible for [Social Security Numbers] and for benefit payments. Continued attention to these issues by both SSA and the Congress is essential to ensure that noncitizens receive benefits to which they are entitled and the integrity of the Social Security program is protected.[133]

At the hearing, testimony was also given by SSA. In addressing the topic of the integrity of foreign data in totalization agreements, an SSA official testified in 2006:

> Under some totalization agreements, SSA and the other country's agency have agreed to use each other's verification of certain eligibility factors, such as a claimant's date of birth. However, this is done only in cases where years of pre-agreement experience and an examination of the other country's system of records during implementation meetings has indicated that evidence from that particular country is accurate and reliable. This policy eliminates the duplication of effort that would result if the agencies of both countries were required to verify the same information.

However, each agreement includes a provision that makes clear that SSA remains the final judge of the probative value of any evidence it receives from any source. SSA is, therefore, able to verify the accuracy of the other country's certification by obtaining original or certified copies of documents and by contacting the claimant directly.

In addition, SSA conducts validation surveys when we become concerned that document fraud may be becoming a problem in a country. Each year we select three countries from a rotating list to conduct "identity and existence" surveys. We train the foreign-service nationals to be vigilant for fraud when examining documents and instruct them to check primary and secondary sources to verify the accuracy of documents.

SSA has recently developed a standardized set of protocols that integrate and formalize the various initiatives we have already undertaken for verifying foreign countries' data. These protocols will be used when negotiating future totalization agreements.[134]

Status of SSA Initiatives in 2009

In October 2009, the Social Security Administration provided information to the Congressional Research Service on the status of key initiatives referenced in the 2005 and 2006 GAO and SSA documents cited in this chapter.

With respect to data exchanges with foreign countries, SSA noted:

> As a result of the success of the regularly recurring death data exchange with Australia, first held in February 2009, SSA has begun discussions with five additional totalization partner countries. SSA pays Social Security benefits to nearly 110,000 beneficiaries in these countries, resulting in nearly $58 million in monthly payments (U.S. dollars). The potential for improved stewardship and reduction of improper payments is significant. These automated exchanges are only possible in countries with which the United States has entered into an agreement. Two additional automated death data exchanges will be piloted before the end of 2009. SSA intends to expand the death data exchange project to all totalization agreement partner countries.

GAO reported that SSA had developed a standardized questionnaire to assess the reliability of earnings data in countries that may be considered for future totalization agreements. Since the agreement with Japan entered into force in October 2005, three totalization agreements have entered into force with Denmark (October 2008), the Czech Republic (January 2009) and Poland (March 2009). SSA indicated that officials in each of these countries provided responses to the standardized questionnaire (SSA's *Systems Security and*

Management Control Environment questionnaire) that were satisfactory to SSA system security reviewers. In addition, SSA indicated that the agency continues to present updated versions of the standardized questionnaire to officials in potential totalization agreement countries when the agency begins exploratory talks on a possible agreement. Foreign officials are informed that SSA can enter into formal negotiations on a totalization agreement only after SSA data security officials "(1) review questionnaire responses, and (2) confirm that they provide sufficient confidence in the reliability and integrity of the foreign nation's system for recording, maintaining, and reporting earnings data in a secure environment, with adequate privacy safeguards for personally identifiable information." Finally, SSA noted that the agency is currently doing an internal review of the standardized questionnaire "to ensure that it continues to elicit the responses necessary for SSA data security authorities to identify and assess the reliability of earnings data in countries under consideration for future [t]otalization agreements."

A GAO official testified in 2006 that SSA was planning further enhancements to the Enumeration at Entry (EaE) program to protect against errors, fraud and abuse. SSA indicated that, among measures taken to protect the integrity of the Social Security Number, the agency has expanded the EaE program, effective August 31, 2009, to make it available to all persons entering the country as lawful permanent residents. Previously, the EaE program was available only to persons over the age of 18 entering the country as lawful permanent residents. Currently, a person of any age who applies for an immigrant visa may elect on the visa application to receive an SSN through the EaE program. SSA noted that "EaE improves the integrity of our enumeration process because the information needed to assign the SSN is collected and verified by the [f]ederal agencies responsible for conferring immigrant status. [The Department of] State certifies the identity and age of the person at the time he or she files for the immigrant visa, and [the Department of Homeland Security] admits the person to the United States as a lawful permanent resident, certifying that the person is authorized to work in the United States."[135]

The Role of Congress

Some policymakers have expressed concerns about the role of Congress in the approval process for international Social Security agreements. The Social Security Act specifies that an agreement will become effective unless the

House of Representatives or the Senate adopts a resolution of disapproval during a period of 60 session days after the agreement is transmitted to Congress for review. [136] As described in detail above, the congressional review process under current law does not provide an opportunity for Congress to amend the text of an agreement. Moreover, an attempt by Congress to stop an agreement from taking effect using the disapproval mechanism specified in the Social Security Act could give rise to a judicial challenge, potentially resulting in an invalidation of the disapproval mechanism and a determination that the agreement is effective.[137]

With respect to reporting requirements, the Social Security Act specifies only that the agreement shall be transmitted by the President to Congress "together with a report on the estimated number of individuals who will be affected by the agreement and the effect of the agreement on the estimated income and expenditures of the programs established by this Act."[138] In 2005, GAO recommended that "reports of proposed agreements be enhanced to make them more consistent and informative and that SSA establish a regular process to reassess the accuracy of its actuarial estimates."[139] In addition, Members of Congress have introduced legislation that would, among other changes, establish new reporting requirements and mandate periodic evaluation of Social Security agreements once they are in force.

LEGISLATION IN THE 111TH CONGRESS

In recent years, legislation has been introduced that would alter the congressional review process for international Social Security agreements, among other changes. For example, in the 111th Congress, S. 42 (Social Security Totalization Agreement Reform Act of 2009 or STAR Act)[140] would require both Houses of Congress to approve a totalization agreement before it could go into effect. In addition, the measure would establish new reporting requirements. S. 42 would require the President to submit the "final legal text" of an agreement to Congress, along with a report containing specified information such as "an assessment of the integrity of the retirement data and records (including birth, death, and marriage records) of the other country that is the subject of the agreement" and "an assessment of the ability of such country to track and monitor recipients of benefits under such agreement." In addition, the Commissioner of Social Security would be required to report to Congress and the Comptroller General of the United States (the Government

Accountability Office) on the impact of a totalization agreement every two years after it goes into effect. With respect to the initial biennial report by the Commissioner of Social Security, the Comptroller General would be required to conduct an evaluation of the report (including specified information) and submit a report to Congress on the results of the evaluation.

Other legislation would make structural changes to international Social Security agreements. For example, in the 111th Congress, H.R. 132 (Total Overhaul of Totalization Agreements Law of 2009)[141] would provide for the transfer of Social Security contributions between the United States and an agreement country, rather than allowing individuals to establish entitlement to benefits under each country's Social Security system based on combined work credits.

Under the measure, if a citizen or national of an agreement country, or an individual lawfully admitted to an agreement country for permanent residence, becomes entitled to benefits under the agreement country's Social Security system *and* the individual has at least 6 quarters of coverage under the U.S. system, the Secretary of the Treasury would transfer from the Social Security trust funds to the agreement country an amount equal to the contributions paid in connection with the individual's covered employment in the United States.

Conversely, if a citizen or national of the United States, or an individual lawfully admitted to the United States for permanent residence, becomes entitled to benefits under the U.S. Social Security system *and* the individual has the equivalent of 6 quarters of coverage under an agreement country's Social Security system, the agreement country would pay to the United States an amount equal to the contributions paid in connection with the individual's covered employment in the agreement country.

In addition, H.R. 132 would exclude from the computation of a worker's Social Security benefits any earnings obtained while the worker was neither a citizen or national of the United States nor lawfully admitted for permanent residence in the United States and was not authorized to work in the United States. The exclusion would apply to all such earnings obtained *before, on, or after* the date of enactment of the bill. H.R. 132 would require the Commissioner of Social Security to recompute benefits as needed to carry out this provision, which would affect benefits for months after the date of enactment of the bill.[142]

CONCLUSION

Supporters of international Social Security agreements point to the advantages associated with such agreements, including elimination of dual Social Security taxes on the same earnings, protection of benefits for workers who divide their careers between the United States and a foreign country and increased portability of benefits through the waiver of residency requirements. Supporters also maintain that Social Security agreements can foster international commerce and enhance diplomatic relations.

With respect to some of the issues and concerns that have been raised about the reliability of foreign data used to administer such agreements, SSA noted in October 2009:

> [Since 2005], SSA has made significant advances in this area. SSA now requires, as a prerequisite for entering into formal negotiations on a totalization agreement, a thorough review of the integrity and reliability of foreign data. SSA has established a formal procedure for obtaining the information necessary to assess the integrity and reliability of foreign data relied upon by the United States to administer social security agreements. SSA has also established procedures for reviewing the information obtained and determining whether the foreign data is reliable and secure. SSA has implemented these procedures, and has reviewed the foreign data in question for all social security agreements negotiated since 2005.[143]

Because the agreements impose a cost to the U.S. Social Security system, some policymakers point to the need for greater assurances that data pertaining to noncitizen workers and beneficiaries (including dependents and survivors) relied upon by the United States to administer the agreements are complete and accurate, a condition necessary to protect the Social Security trust funds from improper payments. In addition, some policymakers point to the need for changes in the congressional review process for totalization agreements, enhanced reporting requirements and ongoing evaluation of agreements after they enter into force as reflected in current legislative proposals.

APPENDIX A. COMPUTATION OF THE SOCIAL SECURITY PRIMARY INSURANCE AMOUNT

The Primary Insurance Amount (PIA) is the basic Social Security monthly benefit amount payable to an individual upon entitlement to retirement benefits at the normal retirement age (i.e., the PIA does not reflect any adjustments for early or delayed retirement) or disability benefits. In addition, the PIA is the base amount used to determine monthly benefits payable to family members on the worker's record (such as a spouse or surviving spouse).

Under current law, the PIA is determined by applying a benefit formula to the worker's average lifetime covered earnings. In the first step of the benefit computation, the worker's nominal earnings (up to two calendar years prior to the year of eligibility—for example, earnings prior to the age of 60 in the case of a retirement benefit) are indexed to wage growth to reflect the change in average wages over time. (Earnings in subsequent years are counted at nominal value.) For purposes of computing a basic retirement benefit, the 35 highest years of indexed earnings are then averaged and a monthly amount is computed to determine the worker's Average Indexed Monthly Earnings (AIME). If a worker has fewer than 35 years of covered earnings, years of zero earnings are counted in the computation of the AIME.[144] The benefit formula is then applied to the worker's AIME. The benefit formula that applies to individuals who first become eligible for retirement or disability benefits in 2010, or who die in 2010 before becoming eligible for benefits, is

- 90% of the first $761 of AIME, *plus*
- 32% of AIME over $761 through $4,586, *plus*
- 15% of AIME over $4,586

For example, the PIA for a worker who reaches the age of 62 in 2010, based on an AIME of $5,000, would be $1,971.00. The PIA would be computed as follows:

- 90% x $761 = $684.90, *plus*
- 32% x $3,825 = $1,224.00, *plus*
- 15% x $414 = $62.10

  PIA = $1,971.00

The worker's PIA is based on the benefit formula that applies in the year the worker first becomes *eligible* for benefits (the age of 62 for retired-worker benefits, the year of disability for disabled- worker benefits, or the year of the worker's death for survivor benefits), rather than the first year of benefit receipt. Beginning with the first year of eligibility, the PIA is increased by the annual Social Security cost-of-living adjustment (COLA) for any intervening years between eligibility and benefit receipt. For example, if an individual who first becomes eligible for retired-worker benefits at the age of 62 in 2010 elects to receive benefits at the normal retirement age (of 66 in 2014), the PIA effective at the normal retirement age would be the PIA calculated using the benefit formula for 2010 (shown above) adjusted annually according to the COLA (if any) effective in December 2010, December 2011, December 2012, and December 2013.

The dollar amounts that separate the three brackets of AIME in the benefit formula ($761 and $4,586) are referred to as bend points. Under current law, the bend points are indexed to wage growth on an annual basis to provide stable replacement rates over time for workers with similar earnings patterns. (The replacement rate is based on Social Security benefits in the first year of benefit receipt divided by pre-retirement earnings.) For example, the projected long-range constant replacement rate, based on retirement at the age of 67 in 2030 or later, is 55% for a scaled low earner; 41% for a scaled medium earner; and 27% for a maximum earner.[145]

The percentages that apply to each of the three brackets of AIME in the benefit formula (90%, 32% and 15%) are referred to as formula factors (or replacement factors). The formula factors, which are fixed under current law, are structured so that Social Security benefits replace a greater share of pre-retirement earnings for lower-wage workers compared to higher-wage workers.

APPENDIX B. EXCEPTION COUNTRIES

The following lists of countries, which are subject to change periodically, are taken from the *Electronic Code of Federal Regulations* (*e-CFR*) with data current as of June 1, 2009, and the Social Security Administration's Program Operations Manual System (POMS). The *e-CFR* is available at http://ecfr.gpoaccess.gov/. The POMS are available at *https://secure.ssa.gov /apps10/* poms.nsf/aboutpoms.

Social Insurance or Pension System Countries

Under the alien nonpayment provision, a noncitizen's benefits are suspended if he or she remains outside the United States for more than 6 consecutive months, unless one of several broad exceptions is met. For example, an alien may receive benefits outside the United States if he or she is a citizen of a country that has a social insurance or pension system that pays benefits to eligible U.S. citizens residing outside that country. The following countries meet the social insurance or pension system exception in Section 202(t)(2) of the Social Security Act:

> Albania, Antigua and Barbuda, Argentina, Austria, Bahamas, Barbados, Belgium, Belize, Bolivia, Bosnia-Herzegovina, Brazil, Burkina Faso, Canada, Chile, Colombia, Costa Rica, Cote D'Ivoire, Croatia, Cyprus, Czech Republic, Denmark, Dominica, Dominican Republic, Ecuador, El Salvador, Finland, France, Gabon, Grenada, Guatemala, Guyana, Hungary, Iceland, Jamaica, Jordan, Latvia, Liechtenstein, Lithuania, Luxembourg, Macedonia, Malta, Marshall Islands, Mexico, Federated States of Micronesia, Monaco, Montenegro, Nicaragua, Norway, Palau, Panama, Peru, Philippines, Poland, Portugal, St. Kitts and Nevis, St. Lucia, Samoa, San Marino, Serbia, Slovakia, Slovenia, South Korea, Spain, Sweden, Switzerland, The Netherlands, Trinidad-Tobago, Turkey, United Kingdom, Uruguay, Venezuela (SSA POMS, Section RS 02610.015 (Status of Countries for Applying Exceptions Based on Citizenship), available at https://secure .ssa.gov/apps10/poms.nsf/lnx/ 030261001 5!opendocument)

Treaty Obligation Countries

To receive benefits outside the United States, alien *dependents and survivors* must have lived in the United States previously for at least five years (lawfully or unlawfully), and the family relationship to the worker must have existed during that time. The law provides several broad exceptions to the five-year U.S. residency requirement for alien dependents and survivors. For example, an alien dependent or survivor is exempt from the U.S. residency requirement if he or she is a citizen of a treaty obligation country (i.e., if nonpayment of benefits would be contrary to a treaty between the United States and the individual's country of citizenship). The following countries meet the "treaty obligation" exception in Section 202(t)(3) of the Social Security Act:

Germany, Greece, Ireland, Israel, Italy, Japan, Netherlands* (20 C.F.R. § 404.463)

*The Treaty of Friendship, Commerce, and Navigation now in force between the United States and the Kingdom of the Netherlands creates treaty obligations precluding the application of the alien nonpayment provision to citizens of that country with respect to monthly survivor benefits only.

ACKNOWLEDGMENTS

The author would like to thank Hector L. Ortiz, former CRS intern, for his contribution to this chapter and the Social Security Administration for providing technical comments on a draft of this chapter.

End Notes

[1] The terms "alien" and "noncitizen" are used interchangeably in this chapter. The Immigration and Nationality Act (P.L. 82-414, 1952) defines an alien as "any person not a citizen or national of the United States."

[2] Much of the information in this chapter is based on the Social Security Administration's (SSA) Program Operations Manual System (POMS) available on the web at *https://secure.ssa.gov/apps10/poms.nsf/aboutpoms.* This is a public version of the POMS used by SSA employees to process claims for Social Security benefits. The information in this chapter is intended to provide an overview of international Social Security agreements. It is not intended to encompass all of the detailed rules and policies related to such agreements.

[3] In the United States, the agreements are also known as totalization agreements. Terms such as "international Social Security agreement" and "totalization agreement" are used interchangeably in this chapter.

[4] The limit on wages subject to the Social Security payroll tax is indexed annually to average wage growth (if a Social Security cost-of-living adjustment is payable).

[5] For purposes of the Social Security program, the United States is defined as a geographic area that includes the 50 states, the District of Columbia, the Commonwealth of Puerto Rico, the U.S. Virgin Islands, Guam, the Northern Mariana Islands and American Samoa.

[6] For purposes of the Social Security program, employment is defined in Section 210 of the Social Security Act and self-employment is defined in Section 211 of the Social Security Act.

[7] Social Security Administration, *2009 Social Security/SSI/Medicare Information*, May 14, 2009, available at http://www.socialsecurity.gov/legislation

[8] Section 210 of the Social Security Act.

[9] Social Security Administration, *U.S. International Social Security Agreements*, available at http://www.socialsecurity.gov/international/agreements_overview.html.

[10] The worker is issued a certificate of coverage by SSA or an authorized agency of the foreign country. The purpose of the document is to certify that the worker is subject to Social Security coverage in the issuing country and exempt from coverage in the other country.

[11] The focus of this chapter is on general coverage rules, rather than specific rules under each agreement. For details on the rules of coverage under each agreement, see the information available from the SSA at http://policy.ssa.gov/poms.nsf/links/0302001000.

[12] For example, see the description of coverage rules under the agreement with Denmark at http://policy.ssa.gov/poms.nsf/links/0302002110.

[13] The agreement with Italy, which was the first agreement to be signed, is the only agreement that does not include a detached worker rule.

[14] If the worker is a national of a country other than Italy or the United States, however, the territoriality rule would apply (i.e., the worker would be covered under the system of the country where the work is performed).

[15] SSA POMS, Section RS 02001.270, Exceptions to the General Coverage Rule—U.S. Belgian Agreement, available at http://policy.ssa.gov/poms.nsf/links/0302001270.

[16] SSA POMS, Section RS 02001.110, General Coverage Rule Under the U.S.-German Agreement, available at http://policy.ssa.gov/poms.nsf/links/0302001110; and Section RS 02001.115, Detached Worker Rule Under the U.S.- German Agreement, available at http://policy.ssa.gov/poms.nsf/links/0302001115.

[17] A worker must have at least 6 quarters of coverage and no more than 39 quarters of coverage under the U.S. system to qualify for a totalization benefit. If a worker has 40 or more quarters of coverage under the U.S. system, he or she would qualify for a regular benefit.

[18] A U.S. totalization benefit is prorated to reflect the proportion of the worker's coverage lifetime completed under the U.S. system. A coverage lifetime is defined in the regulations as the worker's benefit computation years (the number of years used to determine the worker's average indexed monthly earnings) under the regular benefit computation process (for example, 35 years in the case of a retirement benefit). For more information, see the section of this chapter titled *Computation of Benefits*. The Social Security contributions paid under a foreign system do not affect the amount of a U.S. totalization benefit. The amount of any benefit payable under a foreign system would depend on the foreign country's program rules and benefit computation methods.

[19] Fewer quarters of coverage may be required for disability and survivor benefits.

[20] Section 223(d) of the Social Security Act defines disability as the inability to engage in any substantial gainful activity by reason of a medically determinable physical or mental impairment expected to result in death or last at least 12 months.

[21] Other eligibility requirements may apply for receipt of SSDI benefits. For more information, see CRS Report RL32279, *Primer on Disability Benefits: Social Security Disability Insurance (SSDI) and Supplemental Security Income (SSI)*, by Scott Szymendera.

[22] All Social Security agreements allow foreign work credits to count toward the minimum coverage requirement for a U.S. Social Security benefit. Conversely, some agreements allow U.S. work credits to count toward the minimum length-of-work requirement for a foreign benefit. Other agreements, however, do not require U.S. work credits to count toward qualifying for a foreign benefit. Rather, the length-of-coverage requirement for the foreign benefit is reduced. For more information, see SSA POMS, Section GN 01701.100, Overview of Totalization Benefits, available at *http://policy.ssa.gov/poms.nsf/links/0201701100.*

[23] For more information, see the "Waiver of the Alien Nonpayment Provision" section of this chapter.

[24] For a discussion of the different types of executive agreements and a comparison with treaties, see the CRS study prepared for the Senate Committee on Foreign Relations, *Treaties and Other International Agreements: The Role of the United States Senate*, S. Prt. 106-71, January 2001, available at http://www.senate.gov/reference/common/faq/ Treaties.htm. In addition, see U.S. Department of State Foreign Affairs Manual Volume 11—Political Affairs, 11 FAM 723, Exercise of the International Agreement Power, available at http://www.state.gov/documents/organization/_883 17.pdf.

[25] For more information, see the "Congressional Review of Agreements" section of this chapter.

[26] U.S. Congress, House Committee on Ways and Means, Subcommittee on Social Security, *International Social Security Agreements Act*, hearing on H.R. 14429, 94th Cong., 2nd sess., August 4, 1976, p. 2 (hereafter referred to as 1976 Hearing on International Social Security Agreements Act).

[27] U.S. Congress, House, *International Agreement with Italy on Social Security*, House Document No. 95-297, 95th Cong., 2nd sess., February 28, 1977, p. 24 (hereafter referred to as House Document No. 95-297).

[28] House Document No. 95-297, p. 27. There were no relevant provisions of statute at the time (i.e., the requirement pre-dates the addition of Section 233 to the Social Security Act).

[29] H.R. 3153 (93rd Congress) made a number of technical and conforming amendments to the Social Security Act that had been omitted in drafting the conference agreement on the Social Security Amendments of 1972 (P.L. 92-603).

[30] For more information on the legislative history of H.R. 3153 (93rd Congress), see CRS Report RL3 0920, *Major Decisions in the House and Senate on Social Security: 1935-2006*, by Gary Sidor.

[31] The Senate provision further specified that for this purpose: "The continuity of a session is broken ... only by an adjournment of the Congress sine die. The days on which either House of the Congress is not in session because of an adjournment of more than 3 days to a day certain shall be excluded in the computation of the 90-day period."

[32] 1976 Hearing on International Social Security Agreements Act, p. 54.

[33] 1976 Hearing on International Social Security Agreements Act, p. 55.

[34] 1976 Hearing on International Social Security Agreements Act, p. 55.

[35] P.L. 95-2 16 specified that the supplement would apply to "an individual who legally resides in the United States."

[36] The worker's PIA is the basic monthly benefit amount before any adjustments are made for early or delayed retirement (for more information on the PIA, see Appendix A to this chapter). The minimum PIA is the smallest monthly benefit amount (before applicable reductions) payable to a worker or used to determine benefits payable to the worker's dependents and survivors. In 1977, the minimum PIA was frozen at $122 per month for workers who became disabled or died after 1978 or who reached the age of 62 after 1983.

[37] Section 317 of P.L. 95-216.

[38] U.S. Congress, Conference Committees, *Social Security Amendments of 1977*, conference report to accompany H.R. 9346, S.Rept. 95-612, 95th Cong., 1st sess., December 14, 1977, pp. 70-71.

[39] Title XXII, Section 2201(b)(12) of P.L. 97-35.

[40] P.L. 97-3 5 eliminated the minimum PIA for persons who become eligible for benefits in January 1982 or later (an exemption for 10 years was provided for certain members of religious orders who have taken a vow of poverty).

[41] Section 326 of P.L. 98-2 1.

[42] In addition to the changes discussed here, minor technical amendments to Section 233 of the Social Security Act were included in P.L. 98-3 69 (1984) and P.L. 103-296 (1994).

[43] U.S. Government Accountability Office, *Social Security Administration: A More Formal Approach Could Enhance SSA 's Ability to Develop and Manage Totalization Agreements*, GAO-05-250, February 2005 (hereafter referred to as 2005 GAO Report).

[44] U.S. General Accounting Office, *Proposed Totalization Agreement with Mexico Presents Unique Challenges*, GAO- 03-993, September 2003, p. 22.

[45] 2005 GAO Report, pp. 10-12.

[46] Information provided by the Social Security Administration to the Congressional Research Service in October 2009. For more information on the SSA questionnaire, see the section of this chapter titled *Status of SSA Initiatives in 2009*.

[47] Information provided by the Social Security Administration to the Congressional Research Service in October 2009.

[48] Information on the Circular 175 Procedure is available from the State Department at http://www.state.gov/s/l/treaty/ c175/. The applicable procedures are referenced in the Code of Federal Regulations (22 C.F.R. § 181.4) and in the U.S. Department of State Foreign Affairs Manual Volume 11 – Political Affairs, 11 FAM 720 (Negotiation and Conclusion), available at http://www.state.gov/documents/organization/88317.pdf.

[49] U.S. Department of State Foreign Affairs Manual Volume 11—Political Affairs, 11 FAM 724.1, Authorization Required to Undertake Negotiations, available at http://www.state.gov/documents/organization/88317.pdf.

[50] The agreement is subject to ratification in the foreign country as well.

[51] For more information on the process for entering into an international Social Security agreement, see *Statement of Martin Gerry, SSA Deputy Commissioner for Disability and Income Security Programs*, Testimony Before the House Committee on Ways and Means, Subcommittee on Social Security, March 2, 2006, available at *http://www.socia lsecurity.gov/legislation*

[52] Section 233(e) of the Social Security Act.

[53] Some international agreements enter into force upon signing. The Case-Zablocki Act (P.L. 92-403; 1 U.S.C. 1 12b, as amended) requires that the text of an international agreement other than a treaty be transmitted to Congress no later than 60 days after the agreement has entered into force. This requirement, however, does not apply to Social Security agreements because they do not enter into force upon signing, but after a mandatory period of review by Congress.

[54] The agreement with Italy (the first agreement which was signed in 1973) and the agreement with Germany (the second agreement which was signed in 1976) were transmitted to Congress almost five years and three years, respectively, after they were signed. These agreements, however, were signed *before* Congress provided the statutory authority for such agreements (Section 233 of the Social Security Act) under the Social Security Amendments of 1977 (P.L. 95-216, which was signed on December 20, 1977). Subsequent to P.L. 95-216, the agreements with Italy and Germany were transmitted to Congress in 1978.

[55] 462 U.S. 919 (1983).

[56] *Id.* Shortly after its decision in *Chadha*, the Court without opinion and with one dissent summarily affirmed lower court opinions that had struck down a two-House legislative veto provision of the Federal Trade Commission Improvements Act, 15 U.S.C. § 57a-1. See *United States Senate* v. *Federal Trade Commission*, 463 U.S. 1216 (1983); *United States House of Representatives* v. *Federal Trade Commission*, 463 U.S. 1216 (1983).

[57] *Chadha*, 462 U.S. at 952.

[58] 462 U.S. at 951.

[59] 462 U.S. at 944-45.

[60] 521 U.S. 898, 918 (1997). *See also, Plaut v. Spendthrift Farm, Inc.*, 514 U.S. 211, 240 (1995) (stating: "[w]e think legislated invalidation of judicial judgments deserves the same categorical treatment accorded by *Chadha* to Congressional invalidation of executive action.").

[61] See, e.g., *Taylor v. Barnhart*, 399 F.3d 891, 894 (8th Cir. 2005) (indicating applicability of the holding in *Chadha* to Section 233(e)(2)).

[62] The unconstitutionality of legislative veto provisions is noted at 42 U.S.C.A. § 433 (2003), where it is further stated that the provisions of § 233(e) are similar to those struck down in *INS v. Chadha*. For a consideration of bicameralism and presentment requirements generally, see CRS Report RL3 0249, *The Separation of Powers Doctrine: An Overview of its Rationale and Application*, by T. J. Halstead.

[63] *Buckley v. Valeo*, 424 U.S. 1, 108 (1976) (quoting *Champlin Refining Co. v. Corporation Commission*, 286 U.S. 210, 234 [1932]).

[64] 460 F.Supp 737 (D. Mass 1978). In *Califano*, the court was referring to 42 U.S.C. § 1303, which states: "[i]f any provision of this chapter, or the application thereof to any person or

circumstance, is held invalid, the remainder of the chapter, and the application of such provision to other persons or circumstances shall not be affected thereby."

[65] In light of the Court's holding in *Chadha*, it is apparent that any congressional action taken to restrict or control executive authority to enter into Social Security agreements, or to invalidate any such agreements, must be accomplished through bicameral passage and presentment to the President. Accordingly, congressional options in this regard would appear to be limited to imposing additional requirements on the adoption of Social Security agreements, restricting authority to enter into such agreements unless approved by both Congress and the President on a case by case basis, or passing a law disapproving a particular agreement before or after it is finalized. See *Chadha*, 462 U.S. at 951. Analysis of legal issues regarding Section 233(e)(2) of the Social Security Act prepared by T.J. Halstead, CRS Specialist in American Law.

[66] CRS study prepared for the Senate Committee on Foreign Relations, *Treaties and Other International Agreements: The Role of the United States Senate*, S. Prt. 106-71, January 2001, pp. 235-238, available at http://www.senate.gov/ reference/common/faq/Treaties.htm.

[67] Section 233(d) of the Social Security Act.

[68] For more information, see SSA POMS, Section GN 01702.510, Disclosure of Information to Totalization Agreement Countries, available at *http://policy.ssa.gov/ poms.nsf/links/0201702510.*

[69] Information provided by the Social Security Administration to the Congressional Research Service in January 2010. General information on the status of Social Security agreements is available on the SSA website at http://www.ssa.gov/ international/status.html. For more information on the Social Security agreement between the United States and Mexico, see CRS Report RL32004, *Social Security Benefits for Noncitizens: Current Policy and Legislation*, by Dawn Nuschler and Alison Siskin.

[70] This information is available at http://www.ssa.gov/international/agreement_descriptions.html.

[71] In December 2007, there were about 50 million Social Security recipients. Therefore, those who received benefits under U.S. Social Security agreements represented about 0.3% of the total. SSA, *Social Security Bulletin, Annual Statistical Supplement, 2008*, Table 5.A1, available at http://www.socialsecurity.gov/policy/docs/statcomps/ supplement/2008/5a.pdf.

[72] Totalization benefits are Social Security benefits based on combined (totalized) U.S. and foreign work credits.

[73] The benefit application process is described in detail in the 2005 GAO Report.

[74] Claims filed at a foreign social security agency generally are referred to a Foreign Service Post, which deals directly with the claimant.

[75] SSA POMS, Section GN 01702.001, SSA's Role in Processing Claims Under Totalization Agreements—General, available at http://policy.ssa.gov/poms.nsf/links/0201702001.

[76] If a claim is filed at a Foreign Service Post, the foreign coverage record is requested before the application is forwarded to OIO.

[77] 2005 GAO Report, p. 8.

[78] If the claim is concurrent with a claim for Supplemental Security Income, a means-tested benefit administered by the Social Security Administration, Disability Determination Services will make the determination of disability. For more information on the routing of claims for U.S. totalization disability benefits and the development of medical evidence in such cases, see SSA POMS, Section GN 01702.400 - Section GN 01702.420. For more information on SSA's disability programs, see CRS Report RL32279, *Primer on Disability Benefits: Social Security Disability Insurance (SSDI) and Supplemental Security Income (SSI)*, by Scott Szymendera.

[79] Under the agreement with Canada, for example, designated border field offices are responsible for liaison activities and final adjudication of claims for U.S. Social Security benefits, unless the claims are received by OIO directly from claimants or from other field offices.

[80] SSA POMS, Section GN 01702.001, SSA's Role in Processing Claims Under Totalization Agreements—General, available at http://policy.ssa.gov/poms.nsf/links/0201702001. For

more detailed information, see SSA POMS, Section GN 01702.000, DO Development and Routing of Totalization Claims, available at http://policy.ssa.gov/poms.nsf/links/0201702000.

[81] The worker's PIA is the basic monthly benefit amount before any adjustments for early or delayed retirement.

[82] For a detailed explanation of the Social Security benefit computation, see **Appendix A** to this chapter.

[83] For example, in the case of a retirement benefit, assume that the worker's theoretical PIA is $1,000 and that he or she has seven years of work (or 28 quarters of coverage) under the U.S. system. The number of benefit computation years is 35 (or 140 calendar quarters), so the pro rata fraction applied to the theoretical PIA is 0.20 (i.e., 28 quarters of coverage divided by 140 calendar quarters). The pro rata PIA is $200 (i.e., $1,000 x 0.20).

[84] For information on the detailed procedures involved in each step, see SSA POMS, Section GN 01701.200, Totalization Computations, available at *http://policy.ssa.gov/poms.nsf/links /0201701200.* In addition, a detailed description of the totalization benefit computation procedure is available in SSA regulations (20 C.F.R. § 404.1918); totalization benefits are computed in this manner unless otherwise specified in an agreement.

[85] A coverage lifetime is defined in the regulations as the worker's benefit computation years (the number of years used to determine the worker's average indexed monthly earnings) under the regular benefit computation process (for example, 35 years in the case of a retirement benefit). For more information on benefit computation years, see **Appendix A** to this chapter.

[86] A worker who has 40 or more quarters of coverage (10 or more years of covered employment) in the United States would qualify for a regular Social Security benefit (assuming all other eligibility requirements are met).

[87] Social Security Administration, *2009 Social Security/SSI/Medicare Information*, May 14, 2009, available at http://www.socialsecurity.gov/legislation

[88] SSA POMS, Section GN 01701.100, Overview of Totalization Benefits, available at http://policy.ssa.gov/poms.nsf/links/0201701100.

[89] SSA POMS, Section GN 01703.270, Processing Cases Where Insured Status is Acquired Based on U.S. Coverage Only, available at *http://policy.ssa.gov/poms.nsf/ links/0201703270.*

[90] A representative payee is a person, agency, organization or institution that is selected by SSA to manage the funds of a beneficiary who is determined to be unable to manage his or her own funds.

[91] For more information on FEQs, including the mailing schedule for various countries, see SSA POMS, Section RS 02655.005, Preparation and Mailing Schedule—Foreign Enforcement Program (FEP), available at http://policy.ssa.gov/poms.nsf/links/0302655005.

[92] 2005 GAO Report, p. 14.

[93] Information provided by the Social Security Administration to the Congressional Research Service in October 2009.

[94] 2005 GAO Report, p. 13.

[95] For the definition of "lawfully present" see Appendix C in CRS Report RL32004, *Social Security Benefits for Noncitizens: Current Policy and Legislation*, by Dawn Nuschler and Alison Siskin. The lawful presence requirement was added by the Personal Responsibility and Work Opportunity Reconciliation Act of 1996 (P.L. 104-193) and the Illegal Immigration Reform and Immigrant Responsibility Act of 1996 (P.L. 104-208). In addition, see the section of this chapter titled "Legislative History of Payment Rules for Noncitizens."

[96] The Social Security Protection Act of 2004 (P.L. 108-203) requires an alien whose application for benefits is based on a Social Security Number (SSN) assigned on or after January 1, 2004, to have work authorization at the time an SSN is assigned, or at some later time, to gain insured status under the Social Security program. An alien whose benefit application is based on an SSN assigned before January 1, 2004, may count all covered earnings toward

insured status, regardless of work authorization. For more information, see CRS Report RL32004, *Social Security Benefits for Noncitizens: Current Policy and Legislation*, by Dawn Nuschler and Alison Siskin.

[97] "Outside the United States" means outside the territorial boundaries of the 50 states, the District of Columbia, the Commonwealth of Puerto Rico, the U.S. Virgin Islands, Guam, the Northern Mariana Islands, and American Samoa.

[98] The 6-month period of absence begins with the first full calendar month following the period in which the individual has been outside the United States for more than 30 consecutive days. If the individual returns to the United States for any part of a day during the 30-day period, the 30-day period starts over.

[99] For information on the alien nonpayment provision, see SSA POMS, Section RS 02610.000, Alien Non-Payment Provisions, available at *http://policy.ssa.gov/poms.nsf/links/0302610000.*

[100] The criteria used to evaluate the social insurance or pension system of a foreign country to determine whether the exception to the alien nonpayment provision applies is available in SSA regulations (20 C.F.R. § 404.463).

[101] Under the agreement with Australia, the United States pays Social Security benefits to an Australian citizen who resides in the United States, Australia, or a third country with which the United States has a totalization agreement. If an Australian citizen resides elsewhere (i.e., in a non-totalization country), he or she is subject to the alien nonpayment provision. The agreement with Denmark contains a similar provision.

[102] Under the agreement with Australia, Australian dependents and survivors who do not reside in the United States, Australia, or a third country with which the United States has a totalization agreement must meet the five-year U.S. residency requirement to receive payments abroad. The agreement with Denmark contains a similar provision.

[103] Social Security Administration, *Your Payments While You Are Outside The United States*, SSA Publication No. 05-10137, June 2009, available at *http://www.ssa.gov/pubs/10137.html#countries;* and 20 C.F.R. § 404.460 based on the *Electronic Code of Federal Regulations* with data current as of June 1, 2009, available at http://ecfr.gpoaccess.gov/. When a beneficiary who is a U.S. citizen or national leaves a country to which payments are restricted due to U.S. Treasury Department regulations and goes to a country where payments can be sent, receipt of benefits may resume and accrued benefits are paid. In this circumstance, accrued benefits are not paid to noncitizens. When a beneficiary, U.S. citizen or noncitizen, leaves a country to which payments are restricted due to SSA restrictions, receipt of benefits may resume and accrued benefits are paid as long as a beneficiary is eligible for the payments and goes to a country where payments can be sent.

[104] One exception would be aliens who are removed on status violations (i.e., removed from the United States because they are illegally present).

[105] U.S. General Accounting Office, *Issues Concerning Social Security Benefits Paid to Aliens*, GAO/HRD-83-32, March 24, 1983, available at http://archive.gao.gov/d40t12/120895.pdf.

[106] CRS Issue Brief IB82001, *Social Security: Alien Beneficiaries*, by David S. Koitz. This out-of-print document is available from the author of this chapter upon request.

[107] Section 401(b)(2) of P.L. 104-193.

[108] Division C of P.L. 104-208.

[109] Examples of a noncovered pension include a state or local government pension based on noncovered employment or a foreign pension based on noncovered employment. Under the WEP, the worker's Social Security benefit is computed using the WEP PIA formula rather than the regular benefit formula. For more information, see CRS Report 98-35, *Social Security: The Windfall Elimination Provision (WEP)*, by Alison M. Shelton.

[110] In some cases, the WEP may apply to U.S. totalization benefits payable for months before January 1995. For more information, see SSA POMS, Sections GN 01701.300 - GN 01701.320.

[111] For more information, see SSA POMS, Section GN 01701.310, Foreign Pensions Based on a Totalization Agreement with the United States—Effect on the Windfall Elimination Provision (WEP), available at http://policy.ssa.gov/poms.nsf/links/0201701310.

[112] The FRA is the age at which unreduced (or full) Social Security retirement benefits are payable. The FRA is increasing gradually from age 65 to age 67 (it will reach the age of 67 for persons born in 1960 or later). For more information, see *The Full Retirement Age is Increasing* at http://www.socialsecurity.gov/pubs/ageincrease.htm.

[113] The RET no longer applies beginning with the month the beneficiary reaches the FRA. The earnings thresholds ($14,160 and $37,680 in 2010) are indexed annually to average wage growth (if a Social Security cost-of-living adjustment is payable). For more information on the RET, see *Exempt Amounts Under the Earnings Test* at *https://www.socialsecurity.gov/OACT/COLA/rtea.html.*

[114] Social Security Administration, *Your Payments While You Are Outside The United States*, SSA Publication No. 05- 10137, June 2009, available at *http://www.ssa.gov/pubs/10137.html#countries.*

[115] SSA POMS, Section GN 01702.515, Applicability of Annual Earnings Test/Foreign Work Test, available at http://policy.ssa.gov/poms.nsf/links/0201702515.

[116] U.S. Department of Health and Human Services, Centers for Medicare and Medicaid Services (CMS), CMS Publication No. 10116, revised August 2008 (hereafter referred to as CMS Publication No. 10116, August 2008).

[117] CMS Publication No. 10116, August 2008.

[118] Medicare HI pays for hospital bills and certain follow-up care. There is no monthly premium for Medicare HI. Medicare benefits are available only in the United States (i.e., Medicare generally does not cover health services outside the United States).

[119] SSA POMS, Section GN 01701.140 (Entitlement to Hospital Insurance (HI) in Totalization Claims), available at http://policy.ssa.gov/poms.nsf/links/0201701140.

[120] For example, a beneficiary may be dually entitled to a totalization benefit based on his or her own work record (a retirement or disability benefit) and a regular benefit based on the work record of a spouse (a spousal benefit).

[121] A totalization beneficiary may continue to work in Social Security-covered employment and obtain enough work credits to become fully insured under the U.S. system without taking into account foreign work credits. In this case, a totalization benefit may be converted to a regular benefit.

[122] While regular benefits generally are higher than totalization benefits, there could be a circumstance in which a regular benefit that is subject to reduction under the windfall elimination provision (WEP) would be lower than a totalization benefit that is exempt from the WEP. See related discussion in the section of this chapter titled *Exemption from the Windfall Elimination Provision.*

[123] Section 1818 of the Social Security Act; and SSA POMS, Section HI 00801.131, Eligibility for Premium-HI, available at http://policy.ssa.gov/poms.nsf/links/0600801131.

[124] Totalization agreements and the payment of Social Security benefits to noncitizens became the focus of policymakers and the public when it was disclosed in 2002 that the United States was negotiating an agreement with Mexico. In many cases, the concerns expressed about an agreement with Mexico are related to the large number of individuals from Mexico estimated to be working in the United States without authorization using false (in some cases stolen) identities and documents, the integrity and reliability of Mexico's data and recordkeeping systems, and the potential for an agreement to create an incentive for more unauthorized workers to enter the United States. For example, see U.S. General Accounting Office, *Social Security: Proposed Totalization Agreement with Mexico Presents Unique Challenges*, GAO-03-993, September 2003; and Center for Immigration Studies, *Social Security 'Totalization' Examining a Lopsided Agreement with Mexico*, by Marti Dinerstein, September 2004. For more information on the agreement with Mexico (which has been

signed but has not entered into force), see CRS Report RL32004, *Social Security Benefits for Noncitizens: Current Policy and Legislation*, by Dawn Nuschler and Alison Siskin.

125 2005 GAO Report, p. 2.

126 2005 GAO Report, p. 3.

127 2005 GAO Report, p. 3.

128 2005 GAO Report, p. 3.

129 2005 GAO Report, p. 20.

130 See SSA POMS, Section GN 00307, Foreign Evidence, available at http://policy.ssa.gov/poms.nsf/links/0200307000.

131 2005 GAO Report, pp. 15-16.

132 U.S. Government Accountability Office, *Social Security Administration: Procedures for Issuing Numbers and Benefits to the Foreign-Born*, GAO-06-253T, March 2, 2006, available at http://www.gao.gov/new.items/d06253t.pdf (hereafter referred to as 2006 GAO Testimony).

133 2006 GAO Testimony, p. 16.

134 *Statement of Martin Gerry, SSA Deputy Commissioner for Disability and Income Security Programs*, Testimony Before the House Committee on Ways and Means, Subcommittee on Social Security, March 2, 2006, available at http://www.socialsecurity.gov/legislation

135 SSA identified a number of measures taken to protect the integrity of the SSN that are not addressed in this chapter. For example, SSA noted that provisions related SSNs and cards in the Intelligence Reform and Terrorism Prevention Act of 2004 (P.L. 108-458), such as independent verification of all birth records presented in support of an application for an original SSN (excluding SSNs assigned through the Enumeration at Birth and Enumeration at Entry programs), have been implemented. In addition, SSA noted that the agency has opened five additional Social Security Card Centers in the United States since the 2006 GAO testimony. SSA pointed out that, because of the specialized expertise of card center employees, "the card centers streamline and improve the integrity and stewardship of the SSN assignment process."

136 Section 233(e)(2) of the Social Security Act.

137 For more information, see the section of this chapter titled "Congressional Review of Agreements."

138 Section 233(e)(1) of the Social Security Act.

139 2005 GAO Report, p. 9.

140 S. 42 was introduced by Senator Ensign on January 6, 2009. There has been no action on the measure.

141 H.R. 132 was introduced by Representative Gallegly on January 6, 2009. There has been no action on the measure.

142 For examples of legislation related to the pending agreement with Mexico (such as Section 526 of P.L. 110-161, The Consolidated Appropriations Act, 2008, that prohibits appropriated funds from being used to administer benefit payments under an agreement with Mexico that would not otherwise be payable), see CRS Report RL32004, *Social Security Benefits for Noncitizens: Current Policy and Legislation*, by Dawn Nuschler and Alison Siskin.

143 Information provided by the Social Security Administration to the Congressional Research Service in October 2009.

144 The number of computation years used to determine a worker's AIME varies, depending on the type of benefit and other factors. The number of computation years is determined based on the number of years elapsing after 1950 (or year of attaining age 21, if later) up to the year the worker attains the age of 62, becomes disabled or dies, minus any "dropout" years. Dropout years exclude the years of lowest earnings from the computation. The law generally provides for 40 computation years with 5 dropout years (for a net of 35 computation years) in retirement and survivor benefit computations and in many disability benefit computations in which the worker is disabled at age 47 or later. For workers

disabled before the age of 47, the number of dropout years varies from one to four, depending on the worker's age and the number of child care dropout years. The minimum number of computation years is two.

[145] A scaled low earner is assumed to have career-average earnings at about 45% of the national average wage index (AWI). A scaled medium earner is assumed to have career-average earnings at about 100% of the AWI. (In 2010, the AWI is an estimated $43,451 based on the intermediate assumptions of the 2009 Social Security Trustees Report.) A maximum earner is assumed to have earnings for each year equal to the Social Security taxable wage base. (In 2010, the Social Security taxable wage base is $106,800.) Social Security Administration, *2009 Social Security/SSI/Medicare Information*, May 14, 2009, available at http://www.socialsecurity.gov/legislation

In: International Social Security: Agreements... ISBN: 978-1-61761-430-9
Editors: Nicole E. Pampino

Chapter 2

SOCIAL SECURITY: YOUR PAYMENTS WHILE YOU ARE OUTSIDE THE UNITED STATES

Social Security Administration

INTRODUCTION

This booklet explains how being outside the United States may affect your Social Security payments. It also tells you what you need to report to us so we can make sure you receive all the Social Security payments you are entitled to. The information on pages 15 and 16 tells what you need to report. Pages 16 and 17 tell you how to report.

WHEN YOU ARE "OUTSIDE THE UNITED STATES"

When we say you are outside the United States, we mean you are **not** in one of the 50 states, the District of Columbia, Puerto Rico, the U.S. Virgin Islands, Guam, the Northern Mariana Islands or American Samoa. Once you have been out of the U.S. for at least 30 days in a row, you are considered to be outside the country until you return and stay in the U.S. for at least 30 days in a row. If you are not a U.S. citizen, you also may have to prove that you were lawfully present in the United States for that 30-day period. For more information, contact the nearest U.S. Embassy, consulate or Social Security office.

What Happens to Your Right to Social Security Payments When You Are Outside the United States

If you are a U .S . citizen, you may receive your Social Security payments outside the United States as long as you are eligible for them.

However, there are certain countries to which we are not allowed to send payments—see pages 13 and 14 .

If you are a citizen of one of the countries listed below, Social Security payments will keep coming no matter how long you stay outside the United States as long as you are eligible for the payments.

- Austria
- Belgium
- Canada
- Chile
- Czech
- Republic
- Finland
- France
- Germany
- Greece
- Ireland
- Israel
- Italy
- Japan
- Korea (South)
- Luxembourg
- Netherlands
- Norway
- Poland
- Portugal

- Spain
- Sweden
- Switzerland
- United Kingdom

(This list of countries is subject to change from time to time. For the latest information, please visit www.socialsecurity.gov/international/ countrylist1 .htm or contact your nearest U.S. Social Security office, U.S. Embassy or consulate.)

If you are a citizen of one of the countries listed below, you also may receive your payments as long as you are outside the United States unless you are receiving your payments as a dependent or survivor . In that case, there are additional requirements you have to meet—see pages 12 and 13.

- Albania
- Antigua and Barbuda
- Argentina
- Bahamas
- Barbados
- Belize
- Bolivia
- Bosnia-Herzegovina
- Brazil
- Burkina Faso
- Colombia
- Costa Rica
- Côte d'Ivoire
- Croatia
- Cyprus
- Dominica
- Dominican Republic
- Ecuador
- El Salvador
- Gabon
- Grenada
- Guatemala
- Guyana
- Hungary

- Iceland
- Jamaica
- Jordan
- Latvia
- Liechtenstein
- Lithuania
- Macedonia
- Malta
- Marshall Islands
- Mexico
- Micronesia, Fed. States of
- Monaco
- Montenegro
- Nicaragua
- Palau
- Panama
- Peru
- Philippines
- St. Kitts and Nevis
- St. Lucia
- Samoa (formerly Western Samoa)
- San Marino
- Serbia
- Slovakia
- Slovenia
- Trinidad-Tobago
- Turkey
- Uruguay
- Venezuela

(This list of countries is subject to change from time to time. For the latest information, please visit www.socialsecurity.gov/international/ countrylist2. htm or contact your nearest U.S. Social Security office, U.S. Embassy or consulate.)

If you are not a U .S . citizen or a citizen of one of the other countries listed on pages 6, 7 and 8, your payments will stop after you have been outside the United States for six full calendar months unless you meet one of the following exceptions:

- You were eligible for monthly Social Security benefits for December 1956; or
- You are in the active military or naval service of the United States; or
- The worker on whose record your benefits are based had railroad work treated as covered employment by the Social Security program; or
- The worker on whose record your benefits are based died while in the U.S. military service or as a result of a service- connected disability and was not dishonorably discharged; or
- You are a resident of a country with which the United States has a Social Security agreement.

Currently, these countries are:

- Australia
- Austria
- Belgium
- Canada
- Chile
- Czech Republic
- Denmark
- Finland
- France
- Germany
- Greece
- Ireland
- Italy
- Japan
- Korea (South)
- Luxembourg
- Netherlands
- Norway
- Poland
- Portugal
- Spain
- Sweden
- Switzerland
- United Kingdom

(This list of countries is subject to change from time to time. For the latest information, please visit www.socialsecurity.gov/international/ countrylist3. htm or contact your nearest U.S. Social Security office, U.S. Embassy or consulate.) However, the agreements with Austria, Belgium, Germany, Sweden and Switzerland permit you to receive benefits as a dependent or survivor of a worker while you reside in the foreign country. This is true only if the worker is (or was at the time of death) a U.S. citizen or a citizen of your country of residence; or

- You are a citizen of one of the countries listed on pages 10 and 11, and the worker on whose record your benefits are based lived in the United States for at least 10 years or earned at least 40 credits under the U.S. Social Security system. If you are receiving benefits as a dependent or survivor, see page 12 for additional requirements.

- Afghanistan
- Australia
- Bangladesh
- Bhutan
- Botswana
- Burma
- Burundi
- Cameroon
- Cape Verde
- Central African Republic
- Chad
- China
- Congo, Rep. of
- Ethiopia
- Fiji
- Gambia
- Ghana
- Haiti
- Honduras
- India
- Indonesia
- Kenya
- Laos

- Lebanon
- Lesotho
- Liberia
- Madagascar
- Malawi
- Malaysia
- Mali
- Mauritania
- Mauritius
- Morocco
- Nepal
- Nigeria
- Pakistan
- St. Vincent & Grenadines
- Senegal
- Sierra Leone
- Singapore
- Solomon Islands
- Somalia
- South Africa
- Sri Lanka
- Sudan
- Swaziland
- Taiwan
- Tanzania
- Thailand
- Togo
- Tonga
- Tunisia
- Uganda
- Yemen

(This list of countries is subject to change from time to time. For the latest information, please visit www.socialsecurity.gov/international/ countrylist4. htm or contact your nearest U.S. Social Security office, U.S. Embassy or consulate.)

If you are not a citizen of one of the countries listed on pages 10 and 11, you cannot use this exception.

If you are not a U.S. citizen and none of these exceptions applies to you, your payments will stop after you have been outside the United States for six full months. Once this happens, your payments cannot be started again until you come back and stay in the United States for a whole calendar month. You have to be in the United States on the first minute of the first day of a month and stay through the last minute of the last day of that month. In addition, you may be required to prove that you have been lawfully present in the United States for the full calendar month. For more information, contact the nearest U.S. Embassy, consulate or Social Security office.

Additional Residency Requirements for Dependents and Survivors

If you receive benefits as a dependent or survivor of a worker, special requirements may affect your right to receive Social Security payments while you are outside the United States. If you are not a U.S. citizen, you must have lived in the United States for at least five years. During that five years, the family relationship on which benefits are based must have existed.

Children may meet this residency requirement on their own or may be considered as meeting the residency requirement if it is met by the worker and other parent (if any). However, children adopted outside the United States will not be paid outside the United States, even if the residency requirement is met.

The residency requirement will not apply to you if you meet any of the following conditions:

- You were initially eligible for monthly benefits before January 1, 1985;
- You are entitled on the record of a worker who died while in the U.S. military service or as a result of a service-connected disease or injury;
- You are a citizen of one of the countries listed on page 6; or
- You are a resident of one of the countries with which the United States has a Social Security agreement. These countries are listed on page 9.

Countries to Which We Cannot Send Payments

U .S . Treasury regulations

U.S. Department of the Treasury regulations prohibit sending payments to you if you are in Cuba or North Korea. If you are a U.S. citizen and are in Cuba or North Korea, you can receive all of your withheld payments once you leave that country and go to another country where we can send payments. Generally, if you are not a U.S. citizen, you cannot receive any payments for months in which you live in one of these countries, even if you leave that country and satisfy all other requirements.

Social Security Restrictions

Social Security restrictions prohibit sending payments to individuals in Cambodia, Vietnam or areas that were in the former Soviet Union (other than Armenia, Estonia, Latvia, Lithuania and Russia). Generally, you cannot receive payments while you are in one of these countries, and we cannot send your payments to anyone for you. However, exceptions can be made for certain eligible beneficiaries in countries with Social Security restrictions in place.

To qualify for an exception, you must agree to the conditions of payment. One of the conditions is that you must appear in person at the U.S. Embassy each month to receive your benefits. Contact your nearest U.S. Social Security office, U.S. Embassy or consulate for additional information about these conditions and whether you might qualify for an exception.

If you do not qualify for payment under this procedure, you can receive all of the payments for which you were eligible (but which were withheld because of Social Security restrictions) once you leave that country and go to another country where we can send payments.

What you Need to do to Protect Your Right to Benefits

If you are living outside the United States, periodically we will send you a questionnaire. This lets us figure out if you still are eligible for benefits.

Return the questionnaire to the office that sent it as soon as possible. If you do not, your payments will stop.

In addition to responding to the questionnaire, notify us promptly about changes that could affect your payments. If you fail to report something or deliberately make a false statement, you could be penalized by a fine or imprisonment. You also may lose some of your payments if you do not report changes promptly.

Things That Must be Reported

Listed below are things that must be reported. An explanation of each is given on the page listed.

Page 17	Change of address
Page 18	Work outside the U.S.
Page 23	If you return to work or your disability improves
Page 24	Marriage
Page 24	Divorce or annulment
Page 24	Adoption of a child
Page 25	Child leaves the care of a wife, husband, widow or widower
Page 25	Child nearing age 18 is a full-time student or is disabled
Page 26	Death
Page 26	Inability to manage funds
Page 27	Deportation or removal from the U.S.
Page 27	Changes in parental circumstances
Page 27	Eligibility for a pension from work not covered by Social Security

How to Report

You can report by contacting us in person, by mail or by telephone. If you live in the British Virgin Islands, Canada or Samoa, you can send your report to the nearest U.S. Social Security office. If you live in Mexico, you can send your report to the nearest U.S. Social Security office, U.S. Embassy or consulate. If you live in the Philippines, you can send your report to:

Veterans Affairs Regional Office
SSA Division
1131 Roxas Boulevard
0930 Manila, Philippines

In all other countries, you can send your report to the nearest U.S. Embassy or consulate. Visit www.socialsecurity.gov/foreign for a complete list of these offices.

If you find it easier to contact us by mail, send your report by airmail to the following address:

Social Security Administration
P.O. Box 17769
Baltimore, MD 21235-7769
USA

When you contact us, include the following information:

- Name of person or persons about whom the report is being made;
- What is being reported and the date it happened; and
- The claim number that appears on the letters or other correspondence we send you. (This is a nine-digit number—000-00-0000—followed by a letter or a letter and a number.)

Change of Address

Tell us if your address changes so your checks will not be lost or delayed. Even if your payments are being sent to a bank, report any change in your home address.

When you write to the U.S. Embassy, consulate or the Social Security Administration about a change of address, please type or print your new address carefully and be sure to include the country and ZIP or postal code. Also, be sure to list the names of all your family members who will be moving to the new address.

Work Outside the United States

If you work or own a business outside the United States and are younger than full retirement age, notify the nearest U.S. Embassy, consulate or Social Security office right away. If you do not, it could result in a penalty that could cause the loss of benefits. This loss of benefits is in addition to benefits that may be withheld under one of the work tests explained on the following pages.

For people born in 1937 or earlier, full retirement age is 65. Beginning with people born in 1938, full retirement age increases gradually until it reaches age 67 for those born in 1960 or later.

Report your work even if the job is part-time or you are self- employed. Some examples of the types of work that should be reported are: work as an apprentice, farmer, sales representative, tutor, writer, etc. If you own a business, notify us even if you do not work in the business or receive any income from it.

If a child beneficiary (regardless of age) begins an apprenticeship, notify the nearest U.S. Embassy, consulate or the Social Security Administration. An apprenticeship may be considered work under the Social Security program.

The following work tests may affect the amount of your monthly benefit payment. Work after full retirement age does not affect the payment of benefits.

The foreign work test

Benefits are withheld for each month a beneficiary younger than full retirement age works more than 45 hours outside the United States in employment or self-employment not subject to U.S. Social Security taxes. It does not matter how much was earned or how many hours were worked each day.

A person is considered to be working on any day he or she:

- Works as an employee or self- employed person;
- Has an agreement to work even if he or she does not actually work because of sickness, vacation, etc.; or
- Is the owner or part owner of a trade or business even if he or she does not actually work in the trade or business or receive any income from it.

Generally, if a retired worker's benefits are withheld because of his or her work, no benefits can be paid to anyone else receiving benefits on his or her record for those months. However, the work of others receiving benefits on the worker's record affects only their own benefits.

The annual retirement test

Under certain conditions, work performed outside the United States by U.S. citizens or residents is covered by the U.S. Social Security program. If your work is covered by U.S. Social Security, the same annual retirement test that applies to people in the United States applies to you.

NOTE: *Work by some U.S. citizens and residents outside the United States is exempt from U.S. Social Security as a result of international Social Security agreements the United States has concluded with the following countries:*

- Australia
- Austria
- Belgium
- Canada
- Chile
- Czech Republic
- Denmark
- Finland
- France
- Germany
- Greece
- Ireland
- Italy
- Japan
- Korea (South)
- Luxembourg
- Netherlands
- Norway
- Poland
- Portugal
- Spain
- Sweden
- Switzerland
- United Kingdom

(This list of countries is subject to change from time to time. For the latest information, please visit www.socialsecurity.gov/international/ countrylist5.htm or contact your nearest U.S. Social Security office, U.S. Embassy or consulate.)

If you are working in one of these countries and your earnings are exempt from U.S. Social Security taxes because of the agreement, your benefits will be subject to the foreign work test described on pages 19 and 20. For further information on how your benefits may be affected by an agreement, contact the nearest U.S. Embassy, consulate or Social Security office.

If your work is covered by the U.S. Social Security program, you can receive all benefits due you for the year if your earnings do not exceed the annual exempt amount. This limit changes each year. If you want to know the current limit, ask at any U.S. Embassy, consulate or Social Security office, or write to us at the address shown under "How to report" on page 16.

If your earnings go over the limit, some or all of your benefits will be reduced by your earnings.

- If you are younger than full retirement age, $1 in benefits will be withheld for each $2 in earnings above the limit.
- In the year you reach full retirement age, your benefits will be reduced $1 for every $3 you earn over a different, higher limit until the month you reach full retirement age.

Count your earnings for the whole year in figuring the benefits due you. For most people, this means earnings from January through December.

People who reach full retirement age can receive all of their benefits with no limit on their earnings.

The year your benefits start

In figuring your total earnings for the year in which you first become entitled to benefits, count earnings in that year for months both before and after you became entitled.

The year you reach age 18

Your benefits as a child stop at age 18 unless you are a full-time student in an elementary or secondary school, or you are disabled. Your earnings for the entire year in which you reach age 18 count in figuring the amount of benefits due you for the year regardless of whether your payments continue or stop at age 18.

If you Return to Work or Your Disability Improves

If you receive payments because you are disabled, let us know right away if your condition improves or you go back to work. You can keep receiving payments for up to nine months while you are working. This nine-month period is called a “trial work period.” The trial work period gives you a chance to test whether you are able to work without worrying about having your payments stopped. If, after nine months, you are able to continue working, you will get payments for three more months before they stop.

If you are not able to keep working, you will continue to receive disability benefits.

Marriage

Let us know if anyone receiving benefits gets married. In some cases, Social Security payments stop after marriage. In other cases, the amount of the payments changes. This depends on the kind of benefits received and, sometimes, on whether the person you marry gets payments.

Divorce or Annulment

Notify us if your marriage is annulled or you get a divorce. Divorce or annulment does not necessarily mean that your Social Security payments will stop. If you are receiving payments based on your own work record, divorce or annulment of your marriage will not affect your payments. Also, if you are a spouse age 62 or older and you were married to the worker for 10 years or more, your payments will continue even if you divorce. Contact us if your name has changed so we can show your new name on your payments.

Adoption of a Child

When a child is adopted, let us know the child’s new name, the date of the adoption decree and the adopting parents’ names and addresses.

Child Leaves the Care of a Wife, Husband, Widow or Widower

If you are a wife, husband, widow or widower receiving benefits because you are caring for a child who is under age 16 or who was disabled before age 22, notify us right away if the child leaves your care. If you do not, it could result in a penalty that would cause an additional loss of benefits.

A temporary separation may not affect your benefits as long as you still have parental control over the child. Tell us if there is any change in where you or the child lives, or if you no longer have responsibility for the child. If the child returns to your care, you should tell us that also.

Child Nearing Age 18 is a Full-Time Student or Is Disabled

Payments to a child will stop when the child reaches age 18 unless he or she is unmarried and either disabled or a full-time student at an elementary or secondary school.

If a child age 18 or over is receiving payments as a student, notify us immediately if the student:

- Drops out of school;
- Changes schools;
- Changes from full-time to part- time attendance;
- Is expelled or suspended;
- Is paid by his or her employer for attending school;
- Marries; or
- Begins working.

If a child whose payments were stopped at age 18 becomes disabled before age 22 or is unmarried and enters elementary or secondary school on a full-time basis before age 19, notify us so we can resume sending payments to the child. Also, a disabled child who recovers from a disability can have payments started again if he or she becomes disabled again within seven years.

Death

If a person who receives Social Security benefits dies, a benefit is not payable for the month of death. For example, if a beneficiary died any time in June, the payment dated July (which is payment for June) should be returned to the sender.

Inability to Manage Funds

Some people who receive Social Security payments cannot manage their own funds. The person who takes care of the beneficiary should let us know. We can arrange to send the payments to a relative or other person who can act on behalf of the beneficiary. We call this person a "representative payee."

Deportation or Removal from the United States

If you are deported or removed from the United States for certain reasons, your Social Security benefits are stopped and cannot be started again unless you are lawfully admitted to the United States for permanent residence.

Even if you are deported or removed, your dependents can receive benefits if they are U.S. citizens; or, if not U.S. citizens, they can still receive benefits if they stay in the United States for the **entire** month. But they cannot receive benefits for any month if they spend any part of it outside the United States.

Changes in Parental Circumstances

Payments to a child who is not a U.S. citizen could stop or start when certain changes occur. Let us know when the child's natural, adoptive or stepparent dies, marries or gets a divorce (or annulment), even if that person does not receive Social Security payments.

Eligibility for a Pension from Work Not Covered by Social Security

Your U.S. Social Security benefit may be smaller if you become entitled to a U.S. Social Security retirement or disability benefit and start to receive another monthly pension, such as a foreign social security or private pension, based in whole or in part on work not covered by U.S. Social Security. A different formula may be used to figure your U.S. Social Security benefit. For more information, ask at any U.S. Embassy, consulate or Social Security office for *Windfall Elimination Provision* (Publication No. 05-10045).

If Your Check is Lost or Stolen

It usually takes longer to deliver checks outside the United States. Delivery time varies from country to country and your check may not arrive the same day each month. If you do not receive your check after a reasonable waiting period, or if it is lost or stolen, contact the nearest U.S. Embassy or consulate or write directly to the Social Security Administration. Our address is on page 17.

We will replace your check as soon as possible. But please make every effort to keep your check safe, because it will take some time to replace a check while you are outside the country.

Direct Deposit in Financial Institutions

You may want your Social Security payment to be directly deposited into your account at either a financial institution in the country where you live or a U.S. financial institution. Even if you use the direct deposit service, you must keep us informed of any change in your current residence address.

Direct deposit has several advantages. You never have to worry about your check being delayed in the mail, lost or stolen. With direct deposit you receive your payment much faster than if you are paid by check (usually one to three weeks faster than check deliveries). You also avoid check cashing and currency conversion fees. Some countries where direct deposit payments are available include:

- Anguilla
- Antigua & Barbuda
- Australia
- Austria
- Bahama Islands
- Barbados
- Belgium
- British Virgin Islands
- Canada
- Cayman Islands
- Cyprus
- Denmark
- Dominican Republic
- Finland
- France
- Germany
- Greece
- Grenada
- Haiti
- Hong Kong
- Hungary
- Ireland
- Israel
- Italy
- Jamaica
- Japan
- Malta
- Mexico
- Netherlands
- Netherlands Antilles
- New Zealand
- Norway
- Panama
- Poland
- Portugal
- St. Kitts and Nevis
- St. Lucia
- St. Vincent and the Grenadines

- South Africa
- Spain
- Sweden
- Switzerland
- Trinidad and Tobago
- United Kingdom

(This list of countries is subject to change from time to time. For the latest information, please visit www.socialsecurity.gov/international /countrylist6.htm or contact your nearest U.S. Social Security office, U.S. Embassy or consulate.)

To determine if direct deposit (or other forms of electronic payment) is available in the country where you live—or to sign up for direct deposit—contact the nearest U.S. Embassy, consulate or U.S. Social Security office, or write to the address on page 17.

Taxes

If you are a U.S. citizen or U.S. resident, up to 85 percent of the Social Security benefits you receive may be subject to the federal income tax.

If you file a federal income tax return as an individual and your combined income is $25,000 to $34,000, you may have to pay taxes on up to 50 percent of your Social Security benefits. "Combined income" means your adjusted gross income plus nontaxable interest plus one-half of your Social Security benefits. If your combined income is over $34,000, you may have to pay taxes on up to 85 percent of your Social Security benefits.

If you file a joint tax return, you may have to pay taxes on up to 50 percent of your Social Security benefits if you and your spouse have a combined income of $32,000 to $44,000. If your combined income is over $44,000, you may have to pay taxes on up to 85 percent of your Social Security benefits.

If you are a member of a couple and file a separate return, you probably will pay taxes on your benefits.

If you are not a U.S. citizen or a U.S. resident, federal income taxes will be withheld from your benefits. The tax is 30 percent of 85 percent of your benefit amount.

It will be withheld from the benefits of all nonresident aliens, except those who reside in countries that have tax treaties with the United States that do not permit taxing of U.S. Social Security benefits (or provide for a lower tax rate). The United States has such treaties with Canada, Egypt, Germany, Ireland, Israel, Italy, Japan, Romania, Switzerland and the United Kingdom (defined as England, Scotland, Wales and Northern Ireland). Under the tax treaty with Switzerland, benefits paid to residents of Switzerland who are not U.S. citizens are taxed at a rate of 15 percent. In addition, the Social Security benefits paid to individuals who are both nationals and residents of India are exempt from this tax to the extent that their benefits are based on U.S. federal, state or local government employment. (This list of countries may change from time to time.)

After the end of the year, you will receive a statement showing the amount of benefits you were paid during the year.

Many foreign governments do tax U.S. Social Security benefits. U.S. residents planning to live in another country should contact that country's embassy in Washington, D.C., for information.

Social Security benefits are calculated in U.S. dollars. The benefits are not increased or decreased because of changes in international exchange rates.

What you Need to Know about Medicare

Medicare is a health insurance program for eligible people who are age 65 or older, or disabled. Medicare protection consists of two basic parts: hospital insurance and medical insurance. The hospital insurance part of Medicare pays hospital bills and certain follow-up care after you leave the hospital. Medical insurance helps pay doctor bills and other medical services.

Medicare generally does not cover health services you get outside the United States The hospital insurance part of Medicare is available to you if you return to the United States. No monthly premium is withheld from your benefit payment for this protection.

If you want the medical insurance part of Medicare, you must enroll. There is a monthly premium that normally will be withheld from your payment.

Because Medicare benefits are available only in the United States, it may not be to your advantage to sign up and pay the premium for medical insurance if you will be out of the United States for a long period of time. But you should be aware that your premium, when you do sign up, will be 10 percent higher for each 12-month period you could have been enrolled but were not.

If you already are covered by medical insurance and wish to cancel it, notify us. Medical insurance—and premiums—will continue for one more month after the month you notify us that you wish to cancel.

In: International Social Security: Agreements... ISBN: 978-1-61761-430-9
Editors: Nicole E. Pampino

Chapter 3

THE CANADIAN SAFETY NET FOR THE ELDERLY

Michael Wiseman and Martynas Ycas

SUMMARY

Recently various analysts have called attention to the apparent success of the Canadian social assistance system in reducing poverty among the elderly and have suggested that there may be lessons to be drawn from the Canadian experience that are relevant to the evolution of the U.S. Supplemental Security Income (SSI) program. This article profiles the Canadian system, compares the system to the U.S. SSI program, reviews the consequences for elderly poverty rates, assesses system costs, and then comments on pertinence of the Canadian experience to SSI policy. The Canadian minimum income guarantee for the elderly is substantially more generous than what is provided by the United States, but it is misleading to claim that the Canadian system costs only "slightly more" than the U.S. program. Such a judgment overlooks a key and costly part of the Canadian system, the Old Age Security demogrant. We estimate the total costs to Canada of providing income support for elderly persons receiving a Guaranteed Income Supplement (GIS) in 2004 to be approximately C$ 13.3 billion (roughly US$11.1 billion), slightly more than 1 percent of gross domestic product (GDP) and almost *fourteen times* the U.S. allocation for SSI and food stamps for elderly SSI recipients. The significance of this commitment is underscored when it is recognized that in 2004 Canadian GDP per capita was just 80 percent of the U.S. level. The Canadian example suggests U.S. policymakers consider better integration of SSI with basic Social Security benefits, experimenting with alternatives to restricting SSI eligibility to individuals with very few assets, and reducing barriers to program access.

INTRODUCTION

The future of the U.S. Social Security program continues to be the focus of a public debate compelled by the system's projected insolvency. Although the outcome of the political struggle is difficult to forecast, it is likely that changes made to the Social Security system to address financing will affect the nation's "safety net," or minimum income guarantee, for elderly and disabled people—the Supplemental Security Income (SSI) program. The 2001 report of the President's Commission to Strengthen Social Security acknowledged this connection and recommended that "Social Security reform plans should also encompass reforms in SSI policy, to improve retirement incomes for those persons who might not otherwise attain poverty-level income in old age" (President's Commission 2001, 136). Since the Commission issued its report, several Social Security reform proposals have included provisions aimed at providing a minimum guaranteed benefit for workers with low career earnings. Little has been done, however, to address the connection between a reformed Social Security system and the SSI program in providing income security for the most vulnerable of the elderly.

Recently, various analysts have called attention to the apparent success of the Canadian social assistance system in reducing poverty among the elderly and suggested that there may be lessons to be drawn from the Canadian experience that are relevant to SSI strategy. Timothy Smeeding and Susanna Sandstrom (2004) report, "Canada has managed to achieve much greater poverty reduction among seniors [than has the United States] while spending much less on social retirement programs than other rich countries (and slightly more than the United States)" (p. 11). They recommend considering the integrated Canadian social insurance/ social assistance system "as a model for future United States OASI [Old-Age and Survivors Insurance]-SSI interactions" (p. 12).

Table 1. Poverty Rates Among the Elderly: Percentage of Population Aged 65 or Older with Income Less than 50 Percent of Adjusted National Median Disposable Income for All Persons

Country	Year	Poverty rate
Elderly		
United States	2000	24.7
United Kingdom	1999	20.9
Germany	2000	10.1
Canada	1998	7.8
Sweden	2000	7.7
Italy	2000	13.7
Finland	2000	8.5
Elderly women		
United States	2000	28.6
United Kingdom	1999	26.2
Germany	2000	13.0
Canada	1998	9.6
Sweden	2000	10.3
Italy	2000	16.2
Finland	2000	11.8
Elderly women living alone		
United States	2000	45.5
United Kingdom	1999	40.7
Germany	2000	19.6
Canada	1998	17.7
Sweden as having disposable	2000	16.5
Italy	2000	28.7
Finland	2000	21.2

Source: Adapted from Smeeding and Sandstrom (2004, Table 1).

Note: Household incomes are adjusted to individual equivalence by dividing household income by the square root of household size. See text and Förster (2005).

This recommendation is based on cross-national comparisons using data collected in connection with the Luxembourg Income Study (LIS).[1] An example of these data is reproduced in Table 1. Poverty for this analysis is defined as having disposable income adjusted for family size that is less than 50 percent of the national median. When applying this standard, poverty among the elderly in the United States is the worst among the seven countries listed, and Canada typically ranks first or second.[2] In particular, Smeeding and his colleagues note the apparently superior performance of the Canadian system in reducing poverty rates among elderly women living alone, a growing share of all elderly persons (Smeeding with Williamson 2001, 24; Smeeding 2006a).

This article profiles the Canadian system, compares the system to the U.S. SSI program, reviews the consequences for elderly poverty rates, assesses system costs, and then comments on pertinence of the Canadian experience to SSI policy. Our core argument is that Smeeding and his colleagues are right in judging the Canadian minimum income guarantee to be substantially more generous than what is provided by the United States, but that it is misleading to claim that the Canadian system costs only "slightly more" than the U.S. program. Such a judgment overlooks a key and costly part of the Canadian system, the Old Age Security demogrant.

Canadian Social Security and Social Assistance

Canada uses "social security" as a generic term referring to a wide range of programs dealing with health, education, unemployment, and family and child assistance, as well as old age, disability, and survivors' benefits. Programs specifically providing income support for the aged, disabled, and survivors are collectively called Canada's Public Pensions System.

The Three Components

For the elderly (persons aged 65 or older), Canada's Public Pensions System has three major components. Together they provide benefits intended to "ensure a basic income to all eligible Canadians" (Human Resources and Social Development Canada (HRSDC) 2005b).[3]

The first component is quite similar to what is termed Social Security (the Old-Age, Survivors, and Disability Insurance program) in the United States:

- *Canada Pension Plan (CPP)/Quebec Pension Plan (QPP)* is a compulsory, earnings-related social insurance program providing income for retired and disabled workers and their survivors. Its benefit formula also contains significant flat- rate components for the disabled and survivors under the age of 65.

The second component has no close parallel in the U.S. system:

- *Old Age Security (OAS)* is a nearly universal pension financed from general revenues and paid to almost all Canadians aged 65 or older. The principal exceptions are those who do not meet residency requirements or who have very high taxable incomes.

The third component is an income-tested SSI counterpart:

- *Guaranteed Income Supplement (GIS)* is a non- taxable benefit paid to low- and moderate-income seniors—about one-third of the elderly population. It is a form of guaranteed annual income (benefits are reduced according to other income received). Like the OAS, the GIS is financed from general revenues.

The tabulation shows outlays on all three types of benefits for Canadian fiscal year 2005–2006 (the Canadian fiscal year runs from April 1 through March 31). Unless otherwise noted, the figures that follow are in Canadian dollars (C$); reducing amounts expressed in Canadian dollars by 15 percent to 20 percent gives approximate contemporary U.S. dollar equivalents.[4] Outlays on public retirement benefits in Canada amount to about 4.5 percent of gross domestic product (GDP). Although direct general comparison with the United States is difficult, the combination of OASI and federal SSI payments to the elderly in the country amounts to about 3.6 percent of GDP. What is particularly striking about the Canadian public pensions system is that almost half of benefits—OAS and GIS—is financed from general revenues. In the United States less than 2 percent of costs of publicly provided pensions for the elderly is funded from general revenues.[5]

Benefit	Expenditures
Contributory pensions	
Canada Pension Plan	24,868
Quebec Pension Plan	7,968
Total	32,836
Other benefits	

(Continued)

Old Age Security	23,044
Guaranteed Income Supplement	6,221
Total	29,265
Total outlays	62,101
Gross domestic product (GDP), 2005	1,372,626
Outlays as percentage of GDP	4.52

Source: Human Resources and Social Development Canada (2006b) and Statistics Canada (2008).

Note: In 2005–2006, C$1 .23 § US$1.

The Canada and Quebec Pension Plans

Established in 1966, the Canada Pension Plan and Quebec Pension Plan have paid benefits since late 1967. The CPP serves all parts of Canada outside of Quebec. Its parallel plan, the QPP, was in important ways a model for the CPP and has very similar contribution and benefit provisions. Covered earnings records in both systems are merged at retirement for dual contributors to calculate a single benefit. As a result, for most purposes the two programs can be considered a single system.

The Canada Pension Plan is a form of contributory, earnings-related social insurance.[6] It pays three kinds of benefits:

1. retirement pensions;
2. disability benefits (which include benefits for disabled contributors and benefits for their dependent children); and
3. survivor benefits (which include death benefits, survivors' pensions, and children's benefits).

Only retirement pensions will be discussed here. With very few exceptions, every person in Canada aged 18 or older and aged 69 or younger with earnings must pay into the CPP. Employees and their employers each pay 4.95 percent on annual earnings between the minimum and a set maximum level ("pensionable earnings"). The minimum level is frozen at C$3,500; the maximum for 2006 was C $42,100. The self- employed pay both portions, levied on net business income. All earnings below the maximum are taxed; persons whose annual earnings fall below C$3,500 receive a refund of contributions when filing an income tax return (HRSDC 2006a).

The pensionable earnings maximum level is adjusted each January, based on increases in the average wage. The contributory period begins when the worker reaches age 18 or in January 1966 (the start of the CPP), and it continues until the worker receives a retirement pension, reaches age 70, or dies. Some parts of the contributory period are dropped out of the benefit calculation, including periods with no or lower earnings while raising children younger than age 7; low-earning months after age 65; any month when eligible for a CPP disability pension; and the lowest 15 percent of earning years in the contributory period.

Eighty-six percent of the 6 million-plus CPP/QPP recipients collect retirement benefits, about 7 percent collect survivor benefits, and the remaining recipients are made up of disabled persons or children of the disabled. The normal retirement age is 65; retirement benefits can be taken at age 60 (with actuarial reduction) or delayed to age 70 (with actuarial increase). Maximum retirement benefits equal 25 percent of the contributor's average lifetime covered earnings (indexed by an economy-wide earnings measure). However, since virtually all Canadians aged 65 or older also receive OAS (and sometimes GIS) pensions (discussed below), the maximum retirement income from combined public sources replaces approximately 57 percent of average net earnings, about 10 percent more than the replacement rate for the U.S. Social Security system (OECD 2005, Table 4.2). Benefits are indexed to the Canadian consumer price index (CPI) and adjusted annually.[7]

Old Age Security

The OAS is the oldest component of the retirement income system. After the federal government was empowered by a constitutional amendment to operate a system of old age benefits, it set up the OAS program in 1952. OAS is paid entirely out of general revenues. All legal residents who have lived in Canada for at least 10 years after reaching age 18 are eligible for OAS at age 65. The payment amount is equivalent to about 14 percent of average wages and salaries. It is reduced based on the duration of Canadian residency. Full benefits go to residents of 40 years or more as well as to certain other persons with extended but less than continuous residence in the country.

Receipt of OAS is not conditional on retirement or income. However, the benefit is taxable, and recipients with total net income in excess of a certain amount have their benefit "clawed back" at a 15 percent rate, repaying part or all of their OAS benefit through personal income tax. The threshold where clawback begins is approximately C$62,000, and benefit loss is complete at about C$ 101,000. Only about 5 percent of elderly Canadians lose any of their OAS to taxes (Office of the Chief Actuary 2005, 66).

Guaranteed Income Supplement

Low-income OAS pensioners are eligible for the income-tested Guaranteed Income Supplement, which is legally a part of OAS. As such, its benefits are also paid entirely out of federal general revenues. For persons entitled to a full OAS payment, the maximum monthly GIS benefit is about C$594 for a single individual and C$779 for a couple (married or common law; amounts are for March 2006). For persons not entitled to a full OAS payment, the maximum GIS payment is increased to bring the combination of OAS and GIS payment to an amount equivalent to the same total benefit that would accrue to a person with full OAS entitlement. Combined OAS and GIS benefits for a low-income couple are about the same as the highest CPP/QPP benefit paid; for a single person they are somewhat higher. (Recall that virtually all CPP/QPP beneficiaries also receive OAS, so CPP/QPP recipients have total income greater than those reliant on OAS/GIS alone.) GIS is not subject to the Canadian income tax, but benefits are reduced by 50 percent of the amount of any non-OAS income.[8] No account is taken of assets, except for the income they generate. About one-third of Canadians older than age 65 receive both OAS and at least some GIS (Office of the Chief Actuary 2005, 93).

Both OAS and GIS benefits are price indexed, and payments are adjusted quarterly for inflation.

The Safety Net

For Canadians older than age 64, the combination of the OAS and the GIS is the income of last resort. The combined benefit paid in March 2004 is summarized for singles and couples in Table 2. (For the remainder of the article we use 2004 data to facilitate later comparison of benefits to various measures of poverty.) In addition to this level of assured income, Canadian elderly receive health care largely without charge through a system called, as in the United States, "Medicare." Government funding, mostly paid to private practitioners, covers 95 percent of hospital and doctor costs and about 70 percent of total aggregate health spending (World Health Organization (WHO) 2006, 58).

The process of applying for and receiving OAS/ GIS benefits in Canada is straightforward. Human Resources and Social Development Canada (HRSDC) administers the program; payments are handled by the Canada Revenue Agency (CRA). Residents normally receive an application for CPP/QPP and OAS benefits in the mail 6 months before their 65th birthday. The form includes a preliminary notification of possible GIS eligibility and asks the recipient if he or she is interested in applying for GIS. If the response is yes, the OAS office obtains detailed information on income for the client and mails this for verification. Once the information is returned and accepted, the combined benefit is provided monthly, in most cases by direct deposit. In years subsequent to the initial award, HRSDC obtains income information from the CRA for clients who have filed a tax return. It is not necessary to visit any office at any stage during this process.

Once eligible persons are in the system, benefits are paid monthly on the basis of past income, with over- or underpayments recouped on notification or at subsequent income tax filings. GIS benefits are offset by half of income from sources other than OAS (including the CPP/QPP). On average, a single GIS recipient in 2004 received a combined monthly sum of C$896, about 46 percent of it from GIS. The average married couple's combined payment is C$ 1,478, about 34 percent from GIS (HRSDC 2006b). The integration of GIS with the other systems and delivery through the income tax system leads to, from an American perspective, a very high take-up rate among eligibles.[9]

Table 2. Canadian Safety Net for the Elderly, March 2004 (Canadian Dollars)

Benefit	Recipient	Maximum benefit		Maximum annual income for benefit receipt[a]
		Monthly	Annual	
Old Age Security (OAS)	All recipients	462	5,550	59,790[b]
	Single	550	6,596	18,741
	Couple[c]	716	8,592	35,294
	Single	1,012	12,145	59,790[b]
Combined OAS, GIS	Couple[c]	1,641	19,692	59,790[b]

Source: Human Resources and Social Development Canada (2004).

Note: C$1 .23 § US$1.

a. Maximum annual income figure includes OAS payment(s); only non-OAS income affects the GIS payment.

b. Benefit clawback through income tax system begins at C$59,790.

c. Assumes both receive OAS benefits.

Comparison with Supplemental Security Income

The U.S. safety net for the elderly—Supplemental Security Income—is a "nationwide Federal assistance program . . . that guarantees a minimum level of income for needy aged, blind, or disabled individuals. It acts as a safety net for individuals who have little or no Social Security or other income" (Social Security Administration (SSA) 2006, i). SSI recipients living alone are categorically eligible for food stamps and Medicaid as well. As a result, when considering the safety net, it is appropriate to combine SSI and the Food Stamp Program (FSP) benefit. Because elderly recipients of means-tested benefits in both Canada and the United States receive significant medical benefits and health outcomes are similar (WHO 2006), we ignore this benefit in comparing the two safety nets.

The Federal Benefit Rate and State Supplements

In 2004 the federal SSI benefit rate (FBR) for individuals living independently was $564 per month; the rate for couples was $846. All but six states provided some type of supplement to this benefit for recipients in specific circumstances such as living in a nursing home (SSA 2005b, 5–6). Twenty-four states provided additional cash payments to single individuals and/or couples living independently. These cash supplements ranged from very little ($1.70 per month for individuals in Oregon) to quite substantial ($553 per month for couples in California). Fifty-five percent of all SSI recipients lived in states with a state cash supplement, making it appropriate to include such payments when comparing benefits between countries. Because the FSP benefit is affected by total SSI received, it is necessary to incorporate this interaction.

Chart 1 shows the net supplement paid in January 2004 to individuals and couples living alone in each of the states that supplemented the cash benefit of all elderly SSI recipients living independently. The states are ordered by the additional individual benefit adjusted for food stamp effects. The first category ("All others") covers the 27 states (including the District of Columbia) with no general cash benefit supplement; these states accounted for 44.7 percent of all elderly SSI recipients in 2004. Continuing up the ladder, the median elderly recipient ranked on the basis of total minimum benefit (FBR plus state supplement plus minimum food stamps) lived in Pennsylvania. Slightly more than one-quarter of all elderly SSI recipients lived in California; only Alaska (which is granted exceptional treatment in the FSP) had a higher net supplement. Because of an exception originally granted in 1974 and continued by subsequent legislation, California SSI recipients are ineligible for food stamps because the FSP benefit is "cashed out" in the state supplement (Arnold and Marinacci 2003). This nuance is incorporated in Chart 1 and subsequent calculations.

The Safety Nets Compared

To compare the SSI/FSP benefit with the Canadian OAS/GIS benefit, we convert the Canadian figures to U.S. dollars using the 2004 OECD Purchasing Power Parity (PPP) of C$1.23(US$1). We use the PPP recognizing that there are many problems with international comparison of real purchasing power at low income levels. Indeed, one of the advantages of relative poverty measures is that comparing the proportion of persons with incomes less than half the median—for example, across countries—allows one to avoid identifying just what half the median buys.

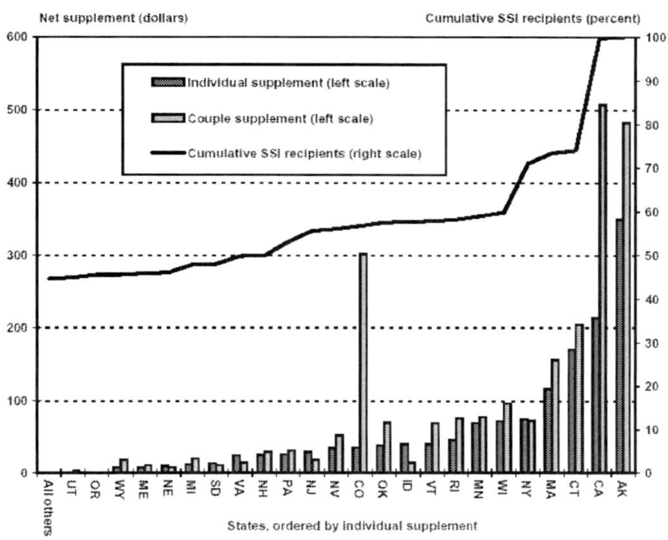

Source: Social Security Administration (2005b).

Chart 1. Monthly state Supplemental Security Income supplements for elderly individuals and couples, 2004

Table 3. Comparison of Safety Nets for the Elderly: Maximum Monthly Benefit, by Marital Status, Spring 2004 (U.S. dollars)

Marital status and benefit	United States SSI/FSP benefit			Canadian OAS/ GIS benefit	
	Supplemental Security Income	Food stamps[a]	Total	Amount	Differential[b] (percent)
States without cash supplement (26)					
Single, average food stamps	564	60	624	823	32
Single, minimum food stamps	564	12	576	823	43
Couple, average food stamps	846	124	970	1,334	37
Couple, minimum food stamps	846	45	891	1,334	50
Pennsylvania (state with median recipient total benefit)					
Single, average food stamps	591	66	657	823	25
Single, minimum food stamps	591	10	601	823	37
Couple, average food stamps	890	109	998	1,334	34
Couple, minimum food stamps	890	32	922	1,334	45
California (highest large-state benefit)					
Single	790	0	790	823	4
Couple	1,399	0	1,399	1,334	-5

Source: Calculations by authors.

Notes: US$1 § C$1.23; OAS = Old Age Security; GIS = Guaranteed Income Supplement; OASDI = Old-Age, Survivors, and Disability Insurance.

a. Minimum food stamp benefit is entitlement given federal benefit rate and state supplement, if available. Average food stamp benefit is calculated as average increment for elderly singles and couples living alone with no income other than SSI/OASDI (see text for source). SSI recipients in California are not eligible for food stamps.

b. Percent by which Canadian benefit exceeds (falls short of, if negative) corresponding amount for United States.

Table 3 presents the combined SSI and FSP benefit for the United States and the corresponding OAS/ GIS benefit for 2004 converted to U.S. dollars. For consistency with our definition of the safety net—the minimum income guarantee—we cite for each state grouping the minimum food stamp entitlement for singles and individuals living alone and dependent wholly on the FBR plus, where available, the state supplement. However, because of housing and medical cost deductions, most elderly SSI recipients receive more than the minimum food stamp amount. To gain a more complete picture of the combined level of support, we have also included an estimate of the mean FSP benefit received by elderly SSI recipients dependent on SSI.[10] The U.S. benefit for states without a state supplement is shown along with comparable calculations for Pennsylvania (the state with the median recipient; see Chart 1) and California. For singles, the Canadian benefit is from 32 percent (with average FSP benefit) to 43 percent (at minimum FSP benefit) greater than the SSI/FSP benefit in states without a supplement; for couples, from 37 percent to 53 percent. Only in California and Alaska do benefits approach Canadian levels.

Compared with payments to couples, the Canadian system treats single adults less generously than do all but the most generous of U.S. states—in general, the benefit for individuals in the United States is a larger fraction of the couples benefit than is true in the Canadian system. As shown in Table 1, the comparatively lower Canadian poverty rates for singles discussed by Timothy Smeeding and Susanna Sandstrom (2004) arise because the level of benefits for both singles and couples in Canada is much greater than in the United States, whether considered in absolute amounts gauged by purchasing power (as in Table 3) or relative to the national median income (as in Table 1).

Both the Canadian and U.S. systems provide for situations in which an eligible individual lives in the same household with a spouse (or, in Canada, a common-law partner) who is ineligible. Here, too, the Canadian system is more generous. In Canada a person aged 60–64 who is partner of a senior OAS/GIS recipient is eligible for an allowance that brings the couple's total income to a level equivalent to what they would receive if both were OAS/GIS recipients. The allowance for a pensioner's survivor younger than age 65 is about 10 percent less than the maximum OAS/GIS benefit for single persons; once reaching age 65 the survivor becomes eligible for full OAS/GIS benefits in her or his own right (Office of the Chief Actuary 2005, 43). In the United States there is no benefit for the survivors of SSI recipients and no complementary benefit for ineligible spouses. Rather, income of ineligible spouses in excess of exclusions that are allowed regular beneficiaries plus a set-aside for a "living allowance" is considered available to the SSI recipient and reduces the SSI benefit (SSA 2006, 13).

Benefits and Poverty

Perception of the consequences of the Canadian system for poverty depends on the standard employed for poverty assessment. Canadians use two methods for assessing poverty—a "low-income cutoff" (LICO) and a "low-income measure" (LIM) (Statistics Canada 2006). Poverty in the United States continues to be officially assessed using a measure originally developed in the early 1960s (Ruggles 1990). A more comprehensive measure proposed in the mid-1990s by a panel convened at the behest of Congress by the National Research Council—an arm of the National Academy of Science—has not been officially adopted (Citro and Michael 1995).

The Low-Income Cutoff and the Low-Income Measure

The low-income cutoff is constructed by determining the income level at which families on average spend 20 percentage points more of their total outlays on necessities—food, clothing, and shelter—than do the average Canadian families with the same number of persons living in the same region and urban/ rural circumstance.[11] In focusing on relative outlays for necessities, construction of the LICO is consistent with the recommendations made for the United States by the National Research Council panel. The standard varies by community size; it is lowest in rural areas and highest in urban areas of 500,000 or more. The cutoffs are reported both before and after income taxes, but both measures include transfers. In 2004 the before-tax LICO for a single adult living in an urban area with a population from 100,000 to 499,999 was C$17,515; for two persons the cutoff was C$21,804. Thus the combined OAS/GIS benefit (see Table 2) fell about 31 percent short of the single-person cutoff and 10 percent below the two-person cutoff. [12]

The low-income measure is based on income alone; this standard is set at 50 percent of median adjusted individual income. Using an equivalence scale, the adjustment—made before calculation of the median— converts each Canadian's family income into the "equivalent" income for a person living alone. The equivalence scale used by Statistics Canada for this purpose assigns a weight of 1.0 to the oldest person in the family, a weight of .4 to the second oldest regardless of age and to all other adults (persons aged 16 or older), and a weight of .3 to any other family members. Thus to find the "individual equivalent" scale for a family of two adults, one would divide whatever family income measure is used by 1 + .4 = 1.4. Once half the median is determined for individuals using this "equilivised" measure as a base, the cutoff is adjusted for larger families by multiplying by the appropriate equivalence weight. The LIM in 2004 was C$ 16,253 before taxes for a single adult and C$22,255 for a couple. The March 2004 OAS/GIS minimum was therefore 75 percent of the LIM for single adults and 87 percent for couples.

Development of the LIM was prompted in part by interest in international comparisons. The LIM standard approximates the measure used by the Organisation for Economic Co-operation and Development (OECD) in some recent comparative poverty studies (Förster and Mira d'Ercole 2005) and in the work of Timothy Smeeding and colleagues, previously cited. The difference between the Canadian measure and that of the OECD is that the OECD equivalence scale is simpler, giving a weight of the square root of family size to each family member. Smeeding uses the square root equivalence scale but focuses on income after taxes, as does the LICO measure that Statistics Canada (2006, 9) "prefers." In practice the choice between the Canadian and square root equivalence scales is of little consequence for most outcomes: Note that both the Canadian and square root scales assume that two-adult households require 1.4 times as much income to achieve the same living standard as a single adult living alone. For purposes of this article, we refer to the square root equivalence scale as the OECD scale, recognizing that some OECD work involves more elaborate adjustments (Förster 2005).

No distinction is drawn among adults on the basis of age in calculating poverty thresholds for the LICO, the LIM, or the OECD scale.

Direct Benefits Comparison with the United States

Table 4 considers the difference between Canada and the United States from the perspective of the poverty measures. We report U.S. figures for Pennsylvania, given that state's "median" status (see Chart 1), and we assume that the SSI recipient receives the average food stamp benefit (see Table 3). The first line of data in Table 4 shows that the Canadian basic income guarantee for the elderly substantially exceeds that provided in the United States. In the second line we report for the United States the OECD poverty standard of 50 percent of median adjusted income, expressed in terms of gross income before taxes but including cash transfers.[13] Using the Canadian equivalence scale, the couple value is 1.4 times the single adult value. The Canadian LIM is taken from official sources and converted to U.S. dollars using the same purchasing power adjustment as that applied in Table 3. Real income is lower in Canada, and half the median—the OECD relative poverty measure—is about 3 percent lower. We also include, in line three, the official U.S. poverty measure, based on the cost in current prices of a yardstick outlay established in 1963. Having established these points of reference, data lines four and five report the maximum benefit in both countries as a percentage of (1) the 50-percent-of-median standard and (2) the U.S. poverty standard, that is, the numbers appearing in lines two and three.

Clearly, by both Canadian and U.S. standards,[14] the Canadian system is significantly more generous than its American counterpart. This generosity extends beyond the minimum guarantee. Every dollar in income from social insurance above $20 reduces the SSI payment by a dollar, but in Canada GIS benefits are "taxed" at only a 50 percent rate. The 50 percent disregard leads to a high proportion of Canadian GIS recipients who also have some income from the Canadian Pension Plan or its Quebec equivalent—83 percent in 2003 (unpublished data provided by the Canada Department of Human Resources and Social Development). It is the combination of a high basic benefit with substantial disregard of other pension income that lifts so many elderly Canadians above the poverty thresholds. The fixed and small SSI disregard produces substantially less mixing: Fifty-seven percent of elderly U.S. SSI recipients had some income from Social Security in December 2004 (calculated from data in SSA (2005a, Table 8)). Social assistance generosity is more than a matter of cash or disregards: Apart from the differences in benefits and treatment of other income, differences in prevalence of poverty in Canada and in the United States may also result from differences in ease of access to the respective safety net systems. It appears to be mechanically much easier to establish OAS/GIS eligibility than it is to initiate and sustain SSI/FSP payments, and GIS has no assets test.

We conclude that the reason why poverty rates are so low in Canada is that the Canadian system is very generous to those with few other resources, and this reduces poverty. Solvency for the self-funding part of the program is less of a problem because almost half of total pension costs comes from general revenues. If a country redistributes more and concentrates this redistribution on the elderly, the relative incomes of elderly people rise, and poverty falls. It is not "rocket science." It is arithmetic.

Looking South

If the redistribution of general revenues is concentrated more on the elderly, the arithmetic is expensive— Smeeding and Sandstrom's assertion that Canada spends "slightly more" than the United States is far from the mark. What would it in fact cost to move SSI for the elderly to something like the Canadian safety net? A first estimate is evident from the last column in Table 3: Increase SSI benefits by 25 percent for singles, 34 percent for couples, and some comparable amount for persons living with others, and disregard more Social Security income in benefit calculation. But this estimate ignores the consequent reduction in FSP benefits, and real emulation of Canada would require elimination of the SSI assets test as well. Both an increase in benefits and elimination of the assets test would raise SSI take-up. Thus for a first estimate, suppose the United States attempts to somehow simply "fill the gap" between current incomes of the elderly and the amount needed to achieve an income equal to the same percentage of median income as that achieved by Canada's current maximum benefit—that is, 75 percent for singles and 87 percent for couples (see Table 4). Depending on certain assumptions about income underreporting in the U.S. Census Bureau's Current Population Survey (CPS), filling the gap would require increasing SSI payments to the elderly by at least 110 percent and possibly as much as 150 percent.[15] Refinement of this "back of the envelope" calculation requires making assumptions about state supplements, the consequences of expansion of eligibility for take-up and private saving, and the implications for related programs like Medicaid. The "possibly as much as" concept seems likely. Costs would multiply further if the same adjustments were extended to nonelderly SSI recipients.

An alternative perspective is to consider the cost of the U.S. and Canadian systems in relation to gross domestic product. Suppose the United States was to devote the same fiscal effort to establishing a minimum income for the elderly as does Canada. What would be the cost? The tabulation on the next page provides a rough cut at comparing the fiscal commitment involved in the Canadian system compared with the cost of SSI.[16]

Combined federal and state SSI costs for elderly recipients amounted to about $8.3 billion in calendar year 2004 (SSA 2006, Table IV.C1 and IV.C4; state supplements for blind or disabled elderly estimated by authors). Food stamp outlays for this group are not published by the U.S. Department of Agriculture. We estimate benefits accruing to elderly SSI recipients using data from the Food Stamp Program Quality Control Database for 2004 (Poikolainen and Ewell 2005) under the assumption that FSP benefits are shared equally among all members of a recipient household. A reasonable estimate is that SSI and FSP costs for the elderly amounted to roughly one-thirteenth of 1 percent of GDP.

Table 4. Safety Nets and Poverty Standards for the Elderly in the United States and Canada, by Marital Status, 2004 (U.S. Dollars)

	United States		Canada	
	Single	Couple	Single	Couple
Maximum benefit (annual equivalent)[a]	7,885	11,979	9,874	16,009
OECD/LIM poverty standard[b]	13,620	19,068	13,214	18,499
U.S. official poverty standard[c]	9,060	11,418	9,060	11,418
	Percent			
Maximum benefit as a percentage of OECD/LIM standard	58	63	75	87
Maximum benefit as a percentage of U.S. poverty standard	87	105	109	140

Source: Calculations by authors.

Notes: Elderly family unit consists of all adults older than age 64.

US$1 ≈ C$1 .23; SSI = Supplemental Security Income; FSP = Food Stamp Program; OAS = Old Age Security; GIS = Guaranteed Income Supplement; OECD = Organisation for Economic Co-operation and Development; LIM = low income measure.

a. For the United States, SSI plus FSP in Pennsylvania; for Canada, OAS plus maximum GIS.

b. For the United States, data calculated by the authors using the 2005 Current Population Survey March Supplement; for Canada, data calculated from Statistics Canada (2006, 29).

c. From DeNavas-Walt and others (2005, 45).

At first glance, Canadian outlays for their safety net look comparable to those of the United States but, of course, smaller: C$5.7 billion. However, such a comparison ignores the fact that GIS comes on top of the near-universal and substantial OAS payment. Assuming that every GIS recipient receives average OAS,[17] we estimate the total costs of providing income support for elderly persons receiving GIS in 2004 to be approximately C$ 13.3 billion, slightly more than 1 percent of GDP and almost *fourteen times* the U.S. allocation for the SSI and Food Stamp programs. The significance of this commitment is underscored when it is recognized that in 2004, Canadian GDP per capita (US$32,000) was just 80 percent of the U.S. level.[18] In a sense even the C$ 13.3 billion figure is an understatement; in the absence of OAS far more Canadians would presumably be eligible for GIS. A full accounting of the commitment to providing a minimum income guarantee would include an estimate of the general reduction in GIS obligation that the presence of the OAS demogrant affords.

The tabulation below, which compares fiscal commitment for 2004, shows a problem with international comparisons of benefit systems—failure to consider context. At first glance the benefit cost of the Canadian GIS is similar to U.S. outlays for SSI. But virtually every poor elderly Canadian citizen gets OAS, for which there is no U.S. equivalent. It is true that OAS is not means-tested (aside from the high-end claw- back). But GIS is clearly calibrated within the context of OAS (indeed, it is delivered by the same agency), and it would be misleading not to include both when describing the Canadian minimum income guarantee. To report, as Smeeding and Williamson (2001) have, "a country like Canada has a very efficient income- related lower tier benefit which produces a low poverty rate for a modest level of social expenditure" is to miss the OAS point and surely to mislead readers about the success of targeting in the Canadian system and the costs of its emulation.

	United States (billions, US$)
Gross domestic product (GDP)	11,734.3
Supplemental Security Income	8.3
Food Stamp Program	0.7
Total	9.0
Total as a percentage of GDP	0.077
	Canada (billions, C$)
Gross domestic product	1 ,290.8
Old Age Security	7.6
Guaranteed Income Supplement	5.7
Total	13.3
Total as a percentage of GDP	1.030

Sources: Social Security Administration (2006); Human Resources and Social Development Canada (2005a). See text.

Review of the Canadian system does suggest some changes in the SSI and the Food Stamp programs that would marginally facilitate access and ensure that the lowest-income elderly receive at least the minimum benefit. Ideally, the FSP benefit would be evaluated by local SSA offices in conjunction with SSI benefit review, unifying the application process and reducing FSP administrative costs for states. While at present, SSI applicants can obtain FSP applications at the SSA office and can file initial applications there, establishing and sustaining benefits requires visits to the agency administering

FSP benefits, even for households made up entirely of SSI recipients and therefore categorically eligible. Considerable experimentation with joint processing of SSI and FSP applications has occurred. The results suggest that simplification of FSP benefit calculation and integration with SSI would raise take- up and reduce administrative costs for states (Food and Nutrition Service 2000; Food Research and Action Center 2004).

It is clear that establishing eligibility for the GIS in Canada is simplified by the absence of asset tests; this permits integration with the internal revenue system and the other benefits programs that are conditioned only on income. Although inclusion of the value of some assets in needs assessment is viewed as important in the United States, it might be possible to shift asset assessment from the present all-or-nothing eligibility determination to a sort of quasi-annuitization in which a fraction of the value of counted assets is treated as income in determining the SSI benefit (see Davies, Rupp, and Strand 2004). Such a procedure could have favorable consequences for savings behavior of the near elderly and the elderly themselves, especially if a portion of assets was disregarded altogether in benefits computation. The potential costs of such a change are, of course, difficult to evaluate; Rupp, Strand, and Davies (2001) estimate that completely eliminating the SSI assets test would have increased annual costs by 7.7 percent in 1991.

Both the Canadian OAS/GIS and the U.S. SSI/ FSP systems guarantee minimum incomes that are below the OECD poverty standards, yet poverty rates are much higher in the United States. In part this is because the gap between the maximum system payment and the poverty standard is much greater in the United States (see Table 4). However, the effect of the Canadian system is also enhanced by the substantial disregard of Canadian/Quebec Pension Plan income in calculation of the GIS benefit. This allows the GIS benefit to fill the gap between the poverty line and the combination of pension and OAS benefits for persons with modest pension entitlement. The GIS 50 percent disregard is proportional and is therefore not affected by inflation. In contrast, for SSI only the first $20 of any monthly Social Security payments is disregarded; beyond this level every dollar of income from Social Security counts against the SSI benefit. The $20 disregard has not changed since the inception of the SSI program in 1974. Had the $20 disregard been held constant in real terms, the current value would be approximately four times greater. Regardless of the poverty standard employed, emulation of the Canadian disregard policy would reduce poverty among the elderly in the United States. Nevertheless, such changes would be costly, because every $1 increase in income disregarded in benefit calculation raises costs by at least $ 1—and more if such changes raise program take-up (Davies and others 2001/2002).

In this discussion we have ignored differences in health care available to the elderly in Canada and the United States, arguing that access and outcomes are roughly comparable. Although outcomes may be similar, costs are not. Various recent analyses have demonstrated that while overall spending by the United States on social welfare is comparable to that of other countries, the United States is unique in the share of such outlays devoted to health (Adema and Ladaique 2005). Thus if means could be found to increase the efficiency of health care delivery in the United States to match that of other countries without sacrificing quality, resources might be freed to target the remaining income poverty among older citizens and to address the concerns voiced by the President's Commission to Strengthen Social Security (Garfinkle, Rainwater, and Smeeding 2006).

Notes

Acknowledgments: We are grateful to Del Corrothers, Denis Dubuc, Josée Perreault, Judy Smelters, and other staff of Human Relations and Social Development Canada. We would like to also thank Richard Balkus, Ben Bridges, Richard Chard, Denise Lamaute, Alexi Strand, and Susan Wilschke of the Social Security Administration (SSA) for comments and corrections on earlier drafts and Joyce Nicholas (SSA) for performing many of the calculations herein. Any remaining errors as well as opinions and judgments expressed are our own and do not reflect policy or perception of SSA.

References

Adema, Willem, and Maxime *Ladaique.* (2005). *Net social expenditure*, 2005 edition. OECD Social, Employment, and Migration Working Papers No. 29. Paris, France: Organisation for Economic Co-operation and Development.

Arnold, Autumn & Amy Marinacci. (2003). *Cash-out in California: A history of help and harm*. San Francisco, CA: California Food Policy Advocates. Available at http://www.cfpa.net/CashoutinCA2003.pdf.

Bouchard, Réal. (2007). Canada. In *International perspectives on Social*

Security reform, Rudolph G. Penner, ed. Washington, DC: The Urban Institute.

Canada Pension Plan Investment Board. (2006). *Annual report*. Ottawa, Canada: The Board.

Citro, Constance F. & Robert T. Michael. (1995). *Measuring poverty: A new approach*. Washington, DC: National Academy Press.

Currie, Janet. (2006). The take-up of social benefits. In *Public Policy and the income distribution*, Alan J. Auerbach, David Card, and John M. Quigley, eds., 80–148. New York, NY: Russell Sage Foundation.

Davies, Paul, Minh Huynh, Chad Newcomb, Paul O'Leary, Kalman Rupp & Jim Sears. (2001/2002). Modeling SSI financial eligibility and simulating the effect of policy options. *Social Security Bulletin, 64(2)*, 16–45.

Davies, Paul, Kalman Rupp & Alexander Strand. (2004). The potential of the Supplemental Security Income program to reduce poverty among the elderly. *Journal of Aging and Social Policy, 16(1)*, 21–42.

DeNavas-Walt, Carmen, Bernadette D. Proctor & Cheryl Hill Lee. (2005). *Income, poverty, and health insurance coverage in the United States: 2004*. Current Population Reports, P60-229, Census Bureau. Washington, DC: Government Printing Office. Available at http://www.census.gov/prod/2005pubs/p60-229.pdf.

Felligi, Ivan. (1997). *On poverty and low income. Ottawa, Canada: Statistics Canada*. Available at *http://www .statcan.ca/english/research/ 13F0027XIE/*1 3F0027XIE1999001 .htm.

Food & Nutrition Service. (2000). *Evaluation of SSI/FSP joint processing alternatives demonstration: Final report*. FNS Online. Washington, DC: Department of Agriculture. Available at http://www.fns.usda.gov/oane/menu/published/fsp/FILES/ ProgramOperations/SSI -FSPsum.htm.

[FRAC] Food Research & Action Center. (2004). *A guide to the Supplemental Security Income/Food Stamp Program combined application projects*. Washington, DC: FRAC. Available at www.frac.org/pdf/CAPreport.pdf.

Förster, Michael. (2005). *What are equivalence scales? Paris, France: Organisation for Economic Co-operation and Development*. Available at http://www.oecd.org/ dataoecd/61/52/3 5411111 .pdf.

Förster, Michael & Marco Mira d'Ercole. (2005). *Income distribution and poverty in OECD countries in the second half of the 1990s*. OECD Social, Employment, and Migration Working Papers No. 22. Paris, France: Organisation for Economic Co-operation and Development.

Garfinkel, Irwin, Lee Rainwater & Timothy M. Smeeding. (2006). A re-examination of welfare states and inequality in rich nations: How in-kind transfers and indirect taxes change the story. *Journal of Policy Analysis and Management, 25(4)*, 897–920.

[HRSDC] Human Resources & Social Development Canada. (2004). Income security programs information card. Catalog # ISPB-258-01-04E. Available at http://www.sdc.gc.ca/en/isp/statistics

———. (2005a). *Income security programs information card.* Available *at* http://www.hrsdc.gc.ca/en/isp/statistics *pdf/aprjun05.pdf.*

———. (2005b). *Income security programs: Our profile*. Ottawa, Canada: HRSDC.

———. (2006a). *Canada Pension Plan (CPP)*. Available at http://www.hrsdc.gc.ca/en/isp/cpp/cpptoc.shtml.

———. (2006b). Income security programs information card. Catalog # ISPB-258-01-06E. Available at http://www.sdc .gc.ca/en/isp/statistics

Nicholas, Joyce & Michael Wiseman. (2008). *Supplemental Security Income and elderly poverty. Revised paper prepared for the 29th Annual Research Conference of Association for Public Policy and Management*, Washington, DC (November 8–10, 2007).

Office of the Chief Actuary. (2005). *Actuarial report (7th) on the Old Age Security Program as of 31 December 2003*. Ottawa, Canada: Office of the Superintendent of Financial Institutions Canada.

[OECD] *Organisation for Economic Co-operation & Development. (2005).* Pensions at a glance: Public policies across OECD countries. Paris, France: OECD.

Poikolainen, Anni & Daisy Ewell. (2005). *Technical documentation for the fiscal year 2004 FSPQC database and QC minimodel*. Washington, DC: Mathematica Policy Research, Inc.

Poon, Preston. (2005). Who's missing out on the GIS? *Perspectives on Labour and Income 6(10)*: 5–14. Available at *http://www.statcan.ca/english/freepub/75-001*-XIE/1 1005/high-1 .htm.

President's Commission to Strengthen Social Security. (2001). *Strengthening Social Security and creating personal wealth for all Americans*. Washington, DC: The White House.

Ruggles, Patricia. (1990). Drawing the line: Alternative poverty measures and their implications for public policy. Washington, DC: The Urban Institute.

Rupp, Kalman, Alexi Strand & Paul S. Davies. (2001). *The potential of the Supplemental Security Income program to fight poverty among elderly women*. In The status of women: Facing the facts, forging the future (Proceedings, Sixth Women's Policy Research Conference, Washington, DC, June 8–9. Washington, DC: Institute for Women's Policy Research,

265–269.

Sarney, Mark & Amy M. Prenata. (2001/2002). The Canada Pension Plan's experience with investing its portfolio in equities. *Social Security Bulletin, 64(2)*, 46–56.

Smeeding, Timothy M. (2006a). *Government programs and social outcomes: Comparison of the United States with other rich nations. In Public policy and the income distribution*, Alan J. Auerbach, David Card, and John M. Quigley, eds., 149–218. New York, NY: Russell Sage Foundation.

———. (2006b). Poor people in rich nations: The United States in comparative perspective. *Journal of Economic Perspectives, 20(1),* 69–90.

Smeeding, Timothy M. & James Williamson. (2001). *Income maintenance in old age: What can be learned from cross-national comparisons*. Working Paper No. 2001–11. Boston, MA: Boston College Center for Retirement Research.

Smeeding, Timothy M. & Susanna Sandstrom. (2004). *Poverty and income maintenance in old age: A cross- national view of low income older women*. Working Paper No. 2004–29. Boston, MA: Boston College Center for Retirement Research.

[S SA] Social Security Administration. (2005a). *SSI annual statistical report, 2004*. Washington, DC: Office of Retirement and Disability Policy, Office of Research, Evaluation, and Statistics.

———. (2005b). *State assistance programs for SSI recipients, January 2004*. Washington, DC: Office of Retirement and Disability Policy, Office of Research, Evaluation, and Statistics.

———. (2006). *Annual report of the Supplemental Security Income program, 2006*. Washington, DC: Office of Retirement and Disability Policy, Office of Research, Evaluation, and Statistics.

Statistics Canada. (2006). *Low income cut-offs for 2005 and low income measures for 2004*. Income Research Paper Series 75F0002MIE–No. 004. Ottawa, Canada: Income Statistics Division.

———. (2008). *Gross domestic product, expenditure-based*. Available at http://www40.statcan.ca/l01/cst01/econ04 .htm.

Trenkamp, Brad & Michael Wiseman. (2008). The Food Stamp Program and Supplemental Security Income. *Social Security Bulletin, 67(4)*, 71–87.

[WHO] World Health Organization. (2006). *World health statistics*. Geneva, Switzerland: WHO.

End Notes

[1] The LIS is a remarkable international collaborative effort initiated by Timothy Smeeding to develop and make available to researchers comparable household-level data on individual and family economic circumstance. For detail and multiple examples of LIS-based research, see the project Web site, http://www.lisproject.org/. Other examples of LIS application to poverty analysis appear in Smeeding (2006b).

[2] Others reach the same conclusion. Among the 24 Organisation for Economic Co-operation and Development (OECD) countries in 2000, only Portugal and Mexico had higher rates of elderly poverty than did the United States. See Förster and Mira d'Ercole (2005, Figure 24) for more detail.

[3] When Paul Martin took office as Canadian prime minister in December 2003, the federal government department known as Human Resources Development Canada (HRDC) was split into two new departments: Social Development Canada (SDC) and Human Resources and Skills Development Canada (HRSDC). In February 2006, this change was reversed by the new conservative government of Steven Harper, and SDC and HRSDC were reunited as Human Resources and Social Development Canada (HRSDC). In this article, the source for all recently accessed agency data is cited as HRSDC.

[4] "Equivalent" here means determining what would be required to purchase an amount of consumer goods in the United States equivalent to what the Canadian benefit can buy in Canada. The Purchasing Power Parity measure published by the Organisation for Economic Co-operation and Development (OECD) for 2005 equates 1.21 Canadian dollars (C$) with 1.00 U.S. dollar (US$).

[5] In addition to $5.2 billion for SSI, this calculation counts as public-provided benefit payments to retirees and their dependent spouses and surviving widow(er)s under Old-Age, Survivors, and Disability Insurance (OASDI)— $265 billion, and for railroad retirement—$9 billion.

[6] For an overview of the Canada Pension Plan and the consequences of important reforms introduced in 1997, see Bouchard (2007)

[7] CPP and QPP contributions not immediately required to pay benefits are managed professionally in a portfolio of foreign and domestic assets including private securities (Sarney and Preneta 200 1/2002). Less than a third of CPP assets are government bonds. The 5-year average real rate of return on CPP assets was 5.9 percent in 2006 (see Canada Pension Plan Investment Board (2006) and Bouchard (2007); real return calculated on the basis of the Canadian CPI).

[8] Income accruing to either partner in couples is treated as shared equally, so the benefit reduction rate for individual partners is 25 percent. Office of the Actuary (2005, 40–42) provides details on GIS operation.

[9] Poon (2005) estimates take-up rate for GIS at 86 percent of eligible persons in 2000. Currie (2006, Table 3.1) cites evidence that participation in SSI is below 75 percent.

[10] The increment in income—a result of the FSP benefit— is calculated using data from the fiscal year 2004 Food Stamp Program Quality Control Database (Trenkamp and Wiseman 2008). To provide adequate sample size, the increment for Pennsylvania is calculated using data for New Hampshire, Pennsylvania, and New Jersey; the New Hampshire and New Jersey state supplements are similar in magnitude to Pennsylvania's (see Chart 1). The higher average FSP benefit for singles in Pennsylvania compared with states without a cash supplement is the result of higher average housing costs in Pennsylvania that lead to greater excess shelter cost deductions.

[11] "Family" means "all persons living in the same dwelling and related by blood, marriage, common-law relationship or adoption" (Statistics Canada 2006, 8).

[12] The official position of Statistics Canada is that the LICOs should not be treated as poverty measures, but the nuances of the agency's position are regularly overlooked by both public media and other Canadian government agencies. The Statistics Canada Web site includes

the following statement from the current chief statistician: "In the absence of politically-sanctioned social consensus on who should be regarded as 'poor,' some people and groups have been using the Statistics Canada low-income lines as a de facto definition of poverty. As long as that represents their own considered opinion of how poverty should be defined in Canada, we have no quarrel with them: all of us are free to have our own views. But they certainly do not represent Statistics Canada's views about how poverty should be defined"(Felligi 1997).

[13] We use gross income rather than net income here because it is difficult to compute federal income tax liability using Current Population Survey (CPS) data, and the official U.S. poverty measure, used in line three of Table 4, is also based on gross (that is, pretax, post-cash-transfer) income. The benefits figures listed for the United States include food stamps, yet food stamps are not included in the incomes data used to calculate the OECD/LIM poverty standard nor are food stamps included in income when assessing poverty using the U.S. standard. Inclusion of food stamps would not alter the estimated median for the income distribution because food stamp receipt is concentrated among persons below the median. Most authorities argue that food stamp benefits should be included in income when assessing poverty (Citro and Michael 1995, 67).

[14] The poverty measure proposed by the National Research Council is for income net of taxes and certain other costs but including the value of certain in-kind transfers such as food stamps and rent subsidies. Applying the NRC methodology, for 2004 the standards for adults and couples living alone were $9,252 and $13,045 respectively, below the OECD/LIM cutoff but above the official poverty standard, especially for couples (unpublished estimates provided by the U.S. Census Bureau).

[15] This estimate was constructed using data for 2002 and a version of the CPS, with individual incomes adjusted for missing information and underreporting using Social Security administrative data. The relative poverty standard used reflects the income distribution in 2002. The analysis assumes that state supplement amounts stay constant, and no adjustment is made in either estimate for the impact of SSI expansion on the Food Stamp Program, Medicaid, and other costs. The lower cost estimate is the result of using conservative income replacement and imputation procedures. The higher estimate is the consequence of more liberal adjustment. The adjustment method is discussed in Nicholas and Wiseman (2008).

[16] The Canadian figures in the tabulation are subject to refinement. GIS costs for the year are inflated from published monthly data for March, July, October, and December. We assume that all GIS recipients receive the average OAS payment. We exclude a (relatively) small amount of GIS paid as "allowance" for survivors and certain other individuals, because these persons are not elderly.

[17] The average OAS for 2004 was approximately C$447.

[18] Note that the difference between the United States and Canada in GDP per capita is much greater than the difference in median incomes as reflected in the OECD/LIM halfthe-median poverty standard reported in Table 4. GDP per capita is an average. Income in the United States is much more unequally distributed than is income in Canada; given that the distribution of income is skewed toward higher incomes, the result is that the ratio of average to median income in the United States is much greater than in Canada, and this affects GDP per capita comparisons.

In: International Social Security: Agreements… ISBN: 978-1-61761-430-9
Editors: Nicole E. Pampino

Chapter 4

CHILE'S NEXT GENERATION PENSION REFORM

Barbara E. Kritzer

INTRODUCTION

In 1981, Chile introduced a new system of privately managed individual accounts, also called capitalization, replacing its public pay-as-you-go pension system (PAYG). Since 1990, 10 other countries in the region have adopted some form of what has become known as the "Chilean model": Argentina (1994), Bolivia (1997), Colombia (1993), Costa Rica (1995), Dominican Republic (2003), El Salvador (1998), Mexico (1997), Panama (2008), Peru (1993), and Uruguay (1996).

Over the years, Chile made some major changes to its capitalization system, such as liberalizing investment rules and increasing the type and number of pension funds that a pension fund management company (AFP) must offer its account holders. However, despite these and other changes, a number of policy challenges remain unresolved including large groups of workers who are not covered and irregular worker participation rates, both of which could lead to inadequate retirement benefits. Also, according to international standards, the administrative fees the AFPs are charging account holders are high and could significantly decrease the size of a worker's pension.

Law 20.255 enacted in March 2008 overhauls the individual accounts system and incorporates previously uncovered groups. The law includes measures to provide adequate benefits to a larger portion of the population, ensure more gender equity, encourage greater competition in the pension fund industry, improve the AFP's management of financial risk to increase the return on the workers' contributions, change the rules for financing survivors and disability insurance, establish more opportunities for voluntary savings, and improve financial literacy.

This paper presents a brief overview of Chile's individual account system and the major changes made to it prior to 2007. The paper then focuses on the major policy challenges that have led to additional reforms and summarizes the provisions of Law 20.255 that address many of the system's shortcomings.

System Overview

In 1981, Chile implemented its mandatory individual retirement account system allowing workers to choose between the public PAYG and the privately managed system, except those workers eligible to retire within 5 years. Since December 31, 1982, new entrants to the labor force must join the new capitalization system and set up individual accounts with the AFP of their choice. The public PAYG system is being phased out as the number of beneficiaries declines and is expected to close by 2050.

Workers must contribute 10 percent of their monthly earnings, up to a maximum of 60 Unidades de Fomento (UFs) (US$2,427) per month to their individual accounts.[1] Each month AFPs charge contributors an administrative fee and a premium for survivors and disability insurance: as of September 2008, an average of 0.99 percent of earnings and 1.71 percent of earnings, respectively (SUPEN 2007–2008).

Workers are free to choose any AFP and may change from one AFP to another at any time. Workers may also make voluntary contributions to their individual accounts and to separate, voluntary retirement savings accounts. Employers are not required to contribute to their employees' accounts and participation is voluntary for the self-employed.

An AFP is a private company whose functions are limited to managing pension funds and providing and administering certain pension benefits. AFPs collect workers' contributions, credit them to the workers' accounts, and invest these monies according to regulations set by the government. AFPs also contract with an insurance company to provide survivors and disability insurance for their members. Until July 2008, the Superintendent of Pension Fund Management Companies (SAFP), an autonomous government agency that was associated with the minister of labor and social security, oversaw and licensed AFPs.

At the normal retirement age (65 for men and 60 for women), workers can use the balance in their individual accounts to do one of the following:[2]

- Purchase an immediate annuity to provide the retiree with lifetime benefits.
- Set up programmed withdrawals to provide income over the retiree's expected life span. If the retiree dies early, dependents may inherit the balance in the deceased's individual account.
- Purchase a deferred annuity, which means setting a future date for purchasing an annuity and until that date make programmed withdrawals from the individual account.
- Purchase an immediate annuity with a portion of the funds in the individual account and make programmed withdrawals with the rest of the funds.[3]

Annuities are purchased from an insurance company for an additional administrative fee and most AFPs charge a monthly fee for programmed withdrawals.

Early retirement is permitted for individual retirement account holders under certain conditions, and excess funds can be withdrawn from an individual account for any reason as long as the worker's account balance is sufficient to finance 150 percent of the minimum pension.

Government Guarantees

Account holders who switched from the public PAYG to the individual account system receive a recognition bond at retirement that represents the value of their accrued rights under the old public system. The value of the bond is adjusted annually to changes in the consumer price index and provides 4 percent interest per year beginning on the date the worker enrolled in the new system. The bond is redeemed and added to the mandatory individual account when the worker retires, becomes permanently disabled, or dies. The bond cannot be redeemed at any other time. To date, almost no one has retired with a benefit entirely from an individual account. In addition, the government guarantees retirees a pension up to 45 UFs per month (US$1,813) if their annuity provider goes bankrupt.

The two types of government-guaranteed benefits are gradually being replaced under the new law: the guaranteed minimum pension (MPG) under the capitalization system and means-tested (PASIS) benefits. The MPG has been paid to men aged 65 and women aged 60 with 20 years of contributions to an individual account and whose total income—pension from an individual account plus other sources of income—is below the minimum level set by the government.[4] The MPG is a top-up subsidy that, combined with the retiree's income, reaches the minimum level. For those who have exhausted their funds, the government has provided the entire amount. Retirees who chose the programmed withdrawals option and exhausted their funds by outliving their actuarial life expectancy could also be eligible for the MPG. Disabled workers must have had 10 years of contributions to qualify for the MPG.[5] PASIS benefits were paid to low-income individuals who were either disabled or over the age of 65 and did not qualify for any other type of pension. The recognition bond, MPG, and PASIS have been funded by general revenues.

Survivors and Disability Insurance

An AFP contracts with an insurance company for survivors and disability insurance. Those younger than the normal retirement age (65 for men and 60 for women) who become disabled from an illness or accident not related to work may be eligible for a disability benefit.[6] Certain unemployed workers who become disabled may also be eligible for a disability benefit. The medical commission first determines if the worker's disability is either total, with at least a 66 percent loss of earning capacity, or partial, with at least a 50 percent, but less than 66 percent loss of earning capacity. A temporary disability benefit (either total or partial) is payable for up to 3 years and is financed by the worker's AFP. A higher level of assessment determines if the worker is permanently disabled after 3 years.[7] The funds in a worker's individual account are used to finance the permanent disability benefit.

A monthly disability benefit is equal to 70 percent of the worker's base salary (average monthly wage in the previous 10 years) for total disability and 50 percent for partial disability. If the balance in the individual account is less than the required minimum to finance a total or partial disability benefit, the worker's disability insurance company makes up the difference (SAFP 2007; SSA 2008).

Survivors benefits are payable to a widow, a disabled widower, and children younger than age 18 (age 24 if a student and no age limit if disabled). In some cases, parents of the deceased may receive a survivor benefit. When a retiree dies, if the retiree was receiving an annuity, eligible survivors receive the corresponding survivor annuity. If the deceased retiree was receiving programmed withdrawals, the balance in the individual account is distributed among eligible survivors. If the balance in the deceased's individual account yields a benefit that is lower than the required amount to finance a survivor pension (70 percent of the worker's average salary in the last 10 years before death), the deceased's life insurance makes up the difference (SAFP 2007; SSA 2008).

If the worker dies before retirement, eligible survivors choose whether to receive an annuity or programmed withdrawals.[8] All the deceased's eligible survivors must receive the same type of benefit. If the balance in the deceased's individual account yields a benefit that is lower than the required minimum (70 percent of the worker's average salary in the last 10 years before death), the deceased's life insurance makes up the difference (SAFP 2007; SSA 2008; ISSA 2008).

History of Changes to Investment Rules

As the system has matured, Chile has gradually liberalized AFP investment rules. When individual accounts were first introduced, investments were restricted to government bonds, financial institution bonds, and a limited amount of corporate bonds; investment in foreign securities was prohibited. In 1981, AFPs were permitted to invest only in low-risk domestic instruments and they could have up to 100 percent of their assets in government bonds. By 1985, when the country's capital market began to develop, the limit on government-issued instruments was lowered to 50 percent, and AFPs could invest between 10 percent and 30 percent of assets in some stocks (Berstein and Chumacero 2003). A law implemented in 2002 allows the AFPs to invest more of their portfolios in equities (see Multifunds, below).

For the first 9 years of operation, AFPs were prohibited from investing in foreign assets. By 1996, restrictions were eased and AFPs could invest up to 6 percent of assets in foreign instruments. This limit gradually increased to 30 percent in 2004 and 45 percent in April 2008. The goal of these measures was to allow the AFPs to diversify their portfolios and gradually reduce the concentration in domestic instruments to lessen the impact on the domestic financial market. Increasing the foreign investment limit could also provide a higher rate of return (Berstein and Chumacero 2003; Kritzer 200 1/2002; SSA 2006–2008).

Chart 1 shows the evolution of selected actual pension fund investments since 1981. The relative mix of investments in the combined AFP portfolios has changed dramatically since the program began. Until 2002, the percentage of assets invested in government bonds ranged from a low of 26 percent of investments in 1982 to a high of 47 percent in 1986. In 1992, international investments represented less than 1 percent of AFP assets, and by 2005, that amount had reached about 30 percent.

Multifunds

Pension fund choices have increased. Until 2002, AFPs could offer only one account to a member. The multi- fund law implemented in August 2002 requires each AFP to offer four different types of funds —called Funds B, C, D, and E—with varying degrees of risk. AFPs may also offer a Fund A with up to 80 percent of its assets in equities. The 2002 law permits account holders to allocate their contributions between two different funds within one AFP, in whatever proportion they choose. Table 1 shows that the limits on investment for each type of fund range from 40 percent to 80 percent of assets in equities for Fund A to mainly fixed instruments for Fund E.

Every fund (Funds A–E) managed by an AFP must maintain a minimum and a maximum rate of return calculated to reflect the average performance of that fund category among all the other AFPs over a 3-year period.[9] Each AFP fund must keep 1 percent of the value of its pension fund as a separate reserve fund whose investments are subject to the same rules as those for the pension funds. If any AFP's fund performance falls below the minimum, it must make up the difference from its reserve fund. If an AFP fund exhausts its reserve fund, the government makes up the difference, dissolves the AFP, and transfers the accounts to another AFP (Law 3500).[10]

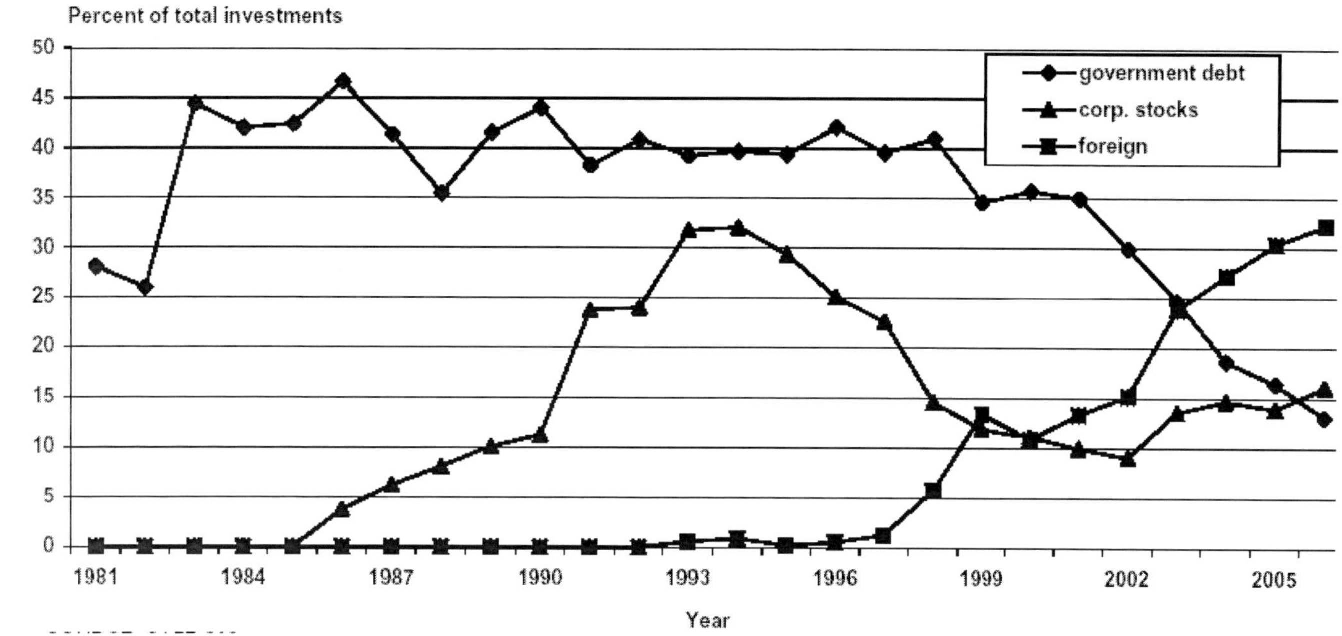

Source: SAFP 2007.

Chart 1. Evolution of selected pension fund investments, by type, 1981–2006

AFP Performance

By the end of 2007, total AFP assets under management reached US$111 billion, about 64 percent of Chile's gross domestic product (AIOS 2007). The historical real rates of return for Fund C, which has been in existence since 1981, have been reported as approximately 10 percent per year. This rate of return includes the high yields within the first 10 years of the program.[11] A recent study found that a worker with average earnings who has contributed regularly since 1981 has earned an average 6.8 percent gross annual real rate of return over the last 10 years (Marcel Commission 2006).

Annuities Law

A law implemented in August 2004 changed the way annuities were sold. Until 2004, individual account holders could purchase an annuity at retirement either directly from an insurance company or through an intermediary. The cost of purchasing an annuity in this way was not regulated and retirees paid fees as high as 6 percent of the value of the annuity (Kritzer 200 1/2002). The 2004 law required AFPs and life insurance companies to create an electronic bidding system for the purchase of annuities, called pensions consultation and offers system (*sistema de consultas y ofertas de montos de pensión* or SCOMP), so that workers nearing retirement can easily compare the products offered by each company. SCOMP is overseen by the Superintendent of AFPs and securities and insurance.[12]

Table 1. Multifunds' Limits on Investment (Percent)

Fund	Limits on investments in equities	
	Minimum	Maximum
Fund A	40	80
Fund B	25	60
Fund C [a]	15	40
Fund D	5	20
Fund E	b	b

Source: SAFP 2007.

a. Formerly fund 1.

b. Mainly fixed instruments.

The 2004 law set a limit on the fees that insurance companies can charge for annuities. Every 2 years, the ministers of labor and social security and finance review the fee caps. Initially, they set the cap at 2.5 percent of the value of the annuity. In 2006, they kept the cap at the same level for the next 2 years.

The annuities law also gradually raised the minimum requirement for an early retirement pension to encourage workers to save more for retirement. In 2004, about half of retirees under the system of individual accounts retired before the normal retirement age. The government was concerned that the earlier workers retire, the more likely it was that over time it would have to supplement a retiree's benefit with the MPG. Under the original rules for early retirement, an individual's pension had to be at least 50 percent of his earnings over the previous 10 years and 110 percent of the current minimum pension. By August 2010, these figures will rise to 70 percent and 150 percent, respectively (Asociación AFP 2004a).

Pension Reform: Policy Challenges and Reform Provisions

Law 20.255 is based largely on the July 2006 President's Pension Advisory Commission Report (Marcel Commission 2006).[13] According to the Commission, the capitalization system is geared toward workers with stable jobs who regularly contribute to an individual account for their entire working lives. The report contends that the system needs to adapt to the changing social conditions in Chile.

The nature of the labor force has been evolving over the past 25 years. Workers are relying less on indefinite labor contracts and more on fixed-term contracts and temporary and part-time jobs. Also, typically, workers in less stable jobs do not regularly contribute to individual accounts. Chile's population is aging and life expectancy is increasing. The population aged 60 or older currently represents 12 percent of the total population and is expected to increase to 17 percent by 2020 and 28 percent by 2050. Since 1980, life expectancy at birth has grown from 70.7 years to 78.5 years and life expectancy at age 60 increased from 16.8 years to 20.7 years for men and 20.2 years to 24 years for women. In addition, more workers are postponing their entrance into the labor force because higher education is available for more individuals aged 15 to 24. As a result, workers are spending fewer years in the accumulation phase for retirement.

The report identified several goals for reforming the 26-year old system of individual accounts including expanding pension coverage, providing an adequate pension, and encouraging competition among the AFPs to lower workers' costs, which would result in a higher net rate of return and a higher pension. This section describes each policy challenge or set of challenges followed by a summary of the reform measure that addresses those issues.[14]

Policy Challenge: Coverage of Workers and Contribution Patterns

A large portion of Chile's labor force has not been covered by any social security program. About 4 million workers, or 61 percent of the labor force, have been covered by either the public PAYG or the individual account system. This figure is about 10 percentage points higher than in 1980 but about the same level as in the mid-1970s, the period just prior to the implementation of the capitalization system (Marcel Commission 2006).

Workers covered by either system include those who do not regularly make contributions because they spend periods of time out of the formal labor force, either in the informal sector or unemployed. While they are in the informal sector or unemployed, they don't contribute to an individual account, which could result in an inadequate pension. Based on their contribution history to date, only a small portion of these workers with an individual account would have enough contributions to qualify for the guaranteed minimum benefit at retirement (Marcel Commission 2006).

Since 1981, the capitalization system has not improved the contribution patterns of workers in the labor force. In 1975, 71 percent of employed workers contributed to the PAYG system and by 1980 that figure had declined to 53 percent (Marcel Commission, 2006). Chart 2 shows that the percent of affiliates (workers with individual accounts) who contributed to their account regularly or sporadically declined from 76 percent in 1983 to 54 percent in 2007 (SAFP 2007; SUPEN 2007–2008). From one month to another, the workers who contribute sporadically are not necessarily the same workers (Arenas de Mesa and others 2006; Berstein, Larrain, and Pino 2006).

Coverage figures for the self-employed, about one- quarter of all workers, are even lower. Their participation has been voluntary and nearly 60 percent have been AFP affiliates. By 2007, close to 40 percent of self-employed affiliates actively contributed to an individual account (Bertranou and Vásquez 2007).[15]

The Social Protection Survey (*Encuesta de Previsión Social* or EPS) conducted by the University of Chile under the aegis of the undersecretary of social security provides a rich source of data for workers' contribution patterns in the capitalization system.[16] A study by several SAFP officials (Berstein, Larrain, and Pino 2006) that links EPS data with administrative data of some 24,000 individuals found that:

- 20 percent of men and women contributed more than 90 percent of the time, and
- 10 percent of men and 20 percent of women contributed less than 10 percent of the time.

The study also shows the percentage of time workers typically spent in the formal and informal labor force. Women had shorter work histories than men, and men were more likely than women to be formal workers with a contract. Workers in the informal sector do not contribute to social security.[17] Since women, on average, spent more than 50 percent of their working lives outside the formal sector, they contributed to their individual accounts less than 50 percent of their potential working lives.

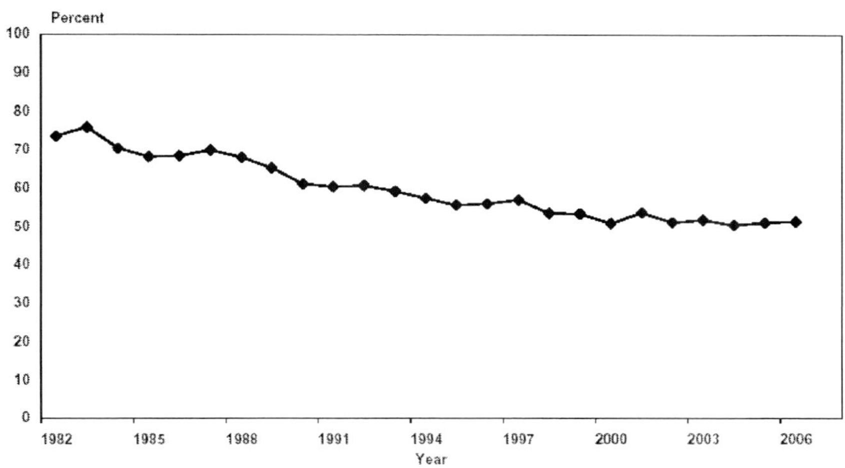

Source: SAFP 2007 and SUPEN 2007–2008.

Chart 2. Percentage of affiliates that contributed to their individual accounts, 1982–2007

The 2006 EPS (which covers the period between 2004 and 2006) found that about half of those surveyed were affiliates. Of the affiliates, men contributed on average about 60 percent of the time and women about 40 percent. Workers contributed about three quarters of the time that they were employed. There was no significant difference between employed men and women. More than 50 percent of those surveyed had worked 100 percent of the time and nearly 25 percent had not worked at all. About 20 percent of the men surveyed were unemployed compared with close to 50 percent of the women (Bravo and others 2008).

Other studies found that workers with higher levels of education and higher income generally contributed more often to social security programs than other groups. The Marcel Commission reported that in Chile about 30 percent of low-income workers contributed to social security, compared to about 70 percent of high- income workers.

Policy Challenge: Pension Adequacy

Even though the Chilean government has provided a guaranteed minimum pension (MPG) to account holders aged 65 or older (men) and aged 60 or older (women) with 20 years of contributions, a large percentage of current workers would not have been eligible for this guarantee.[18] A 2006 study done by several SAFP officials (Berstein, Larrain, and Pino 2006) estimated that, based on the proportion of AFP members who have contributed to an individual account, about 45 percent of them were expected to have a pension that is below MPG and most of this group would not have qualified for the MPG. In 2005, about two-thirds of these workers had fewer than 10 years of contributions. The study predicted that without any changes, by 2025 about 85 percent of these workers would not have enough years of contributions for the MPG.

Pensioners who have chosen the programmed withdrawal option may have been able to receive the MPG when they have exhausted their funds by outliving their actuarial life expectancy. Studies have found that those who choose programmed withdrawal generally have lower account balances than those who choose annuities.[19] As of 2003, about 15 percent of all old-age pensioners with programmed withdrawals were receiving the MPG, compared with 44 percent of disability beneficiaries and 19 percent of survivors (James and Iglesias 2007).

In 2005, an average monthly pension from the individual account system was 131,615 pesos per month (US$252) (SAFP 2007) compared with the minimum monthly wage of 127,500 pesos (US$244) (SAFP 2005–2008). However, it is important to note that to date, almost no one has retired with a benefit that is entirely from the individual account system. A portion of these pensions comes from the recognition bond funded from general revenues that represents the worker's accrued value under the public PAYG system.[20]

If no changes were made to the system, most workers with an individual account who retired between 2020 and 2025 would not receive a benefit equal to about 75 percent of their pre-retirement earnings, the goal of the architects of the system. The Superintendent of AFPs estimated an average replacement rate of 44 percent of earnings for this group of retirees. However, there is a wide variation in the rate when considering gender and educational level. Women with an elementary school education were projected to receive an 11 percent replacement rate and those with a university degree 30 percent compared with 47 percent and 110 percent, respectively, for men (Berstein, Larrain, and Pino 2006).

On the whole, workers who retire early receive a lower benefit than if they would have waited until the normal retirement age (65 for men and 60 for women). As of December 2006, almost half of old-age retirees took early retirement. Close to 70 percent of these early retirees were aged 50 to 59 and about 11 percent were under age 50 (SAFP 2005–2008). A 2004 study by the AFP Association (Asociación AFP 2004a) found that for every year a worker retired early, the worker's pension decreased on average between 7 percent and 10 percent. Between 2002 and 2004, on average, women retired 7 years early and men 9 years early. Some of these workers also withdrew the excess funds from their accounts, which further reduced their benefit. The study concluded that if the early retirees had waited until the normal retirement age and had not withdrawn excess funds, the average pension would have doubled.

Pension Reform: Coverage, Contribution Patterns, and Adequate Pensions

Law 20.255 adds a new pillar, known as Sistema de Pensiones Solidarias (SPS), to the existing mandatory individual accounts system to expand coverage and provide a basic benefit to a larger percentage of the population. As of July 1, 2008, the means-tested (PASIS) pension was replaced with a noncontributory basic solidarity pension called Pensión Básica Solidaria (PBS). This benefit initially covers 40 percent of the poorest individuals in Chile and will be extended gradually to 60 percent of the poorest individuals by 2012. The government estimates that about 600,000 people will be covered in 2008 and by 2012 about 1.3 million people will receive the basic solidarity pension.

The SPS also provides a top-up benefit called Aporte Previsional Solidario (APS) for those individuals who have contributed to an individual account and whose self-financed monthly benefit is between 50,000 pesos (US$97) and 150,000 pesos (US$290) in 2008 gradually rising to 255,000 pesos (US$494) by 2012. Table 2 provides some details about the PBS and the APS (Ministerio del Trabajo y Prevision Social 2008). Pensioners who were receiving the guaranteed minimum pension when the new pillar was implemented on July 1, 2008, may switch to the SPS. Individuals aged 55 or older in March 2008 who will qualify for the guaranteed minimum pension at retirement may also choose between the two types of benefits. Both of these groups may only exercise this option once.

The reform gradually extends mandatory coverage in the individual account system to the self-employed. Their participation is currently voluntary. Beginning January 1, 2012, contributions by the self-employed will be based on 40 percent of taxable earnings, increasing to 100 percent by January 1, 2014. Beginning January 1, 2015, all self-employed will be required to contribute 10 percent of their taxable earnings to an individual account.

Another provision seeks to encourage youth employment and participation in the capitalization system. The measure requires the government to provide a monthly subsidy to low-income workers (those who earn less than one and a half times the minimum wage, 238,500 pesos (US$462) per month in July 2008) between ages 18 and 35 and their employers for the first 24 months of employment after they first enter the labor force. Beginning October 1, 2008, the employer subsidy is equal to half of a contribution to an individual account based on the minimum wage (7,950 pesos (US$15) per month in July 2008) and will be provided each time the worker contributes to an individual account. The workers' contributions are not required to be continual. Beginning July 1, 2011, the subsidy for the low-income workers, the same amount as the employers' subsidy, will be deposited into a worker's individual account each time the worker contributes.

Table 2. Solidarity Pensions System, Requirements, and Benefits

Solidarity pensions system benefit	Eligibility requirements	Monthly benefit
Basic solidarity pension (PBS)	**Old-age pension:** not eligible for any other pension, age 65 or older, lived in Chile for at least 20 years including 4 of the 5 years immediately prior to applying for a benefit.	60,000 pesos (US$116) until 2010; 75,000 pesos (US$145) until 2012
	Disability pension: assessed as disabled by Medical Commission, not eligible for any other pension, age 65 or older, lived in Chile for at least 5 of the 6 years immediately prior to applying for a benefit.	
Social security solidarity contribution (APS)	**Old-age and disability pensions:** must have contributed to an individual acc-ount and have a self-financed pension between 50,000 pesos (US$97) and 70,000 pesos (US$135) a month in 2008, rising to 255,000 pesos (US$494) a month by 2012.	top-up benefit (e.g., up to about 17,000 pesos (US$33) a month in 2008)

Policy Challenge: Toward Gender Equity

Since 1980, the role of women in the family has been affected by the change in structure of a typical household. With the average size of a household decreasing from 4.5 to 3.3 members between 1980 and 2006, the importance of the extended family as a support system has been reduced. Also, between 1992 and 2002, the percent of the population that was married fell from 52 percent to 46 percent. Since 1980, the proportion of one-person households has risen from 7 percent to 13 percent, of which 60 percent are headed by women, who generally have lower earnings, do not qualify for social security benefits, and may not have access to intrafamily transfers (Marcel Commission 2006; Mideplan 2007).

Generally, more men in Chile are in the labor force than women. Chilean women represent 38 percent of the labor force, compared to 44.7 percent in all of Latin America (Umar 2007). Women have shorter work histories than men and men are more likely than women to be formal workers with a contract.

Workers in the informal sector do not contribute to social security. Since women, on average, spend more than 50 percent of their working lives outside the formal sector, they contribute to their individual accounts less than 50 percent of their potential working lives (Berstein, Larrain, and Pino 2006).

A greater proportion of lower income women than men are unemployed, and women tend to work fewer hours in paid labor than men, in part to care for children, older family members, and the household. On the whole, women earn lower salaries than men. According to the latest household survey (CASEN), 29 percent of female workers earn the minimum wage compared with 9.2 percent of male workers. For those with the fewest years of education, men earn close to 25 percent more than women (Marcel Commission 2006; Mideplan 2007). As a result, women have contributed less than men to individual accounts and have had lower account balances, which provide lower retirement benefits.

Since women generally live longer than men, but retire at a younger age and have lower account balances, women's pensions have been between 30 percent to 40 percent less than men's. Also, because companies must use gender-specific mortality tables to calculate annuities, women with the same account balances as men at retirement receive smaller monthly pensions. However, the total value of all future pension payments have been about the same for women and men with the same account balances, since women usually live longer (Marcel Commission 2006).

Under the old rules, married men are required to finance an annuity that provides a survivor benefit to widows; married women have to finance an annuity with survivor benefits only for their disabled husbands. Widows are permitted to receive both a survivor pension and a pension from their own individual account.

Pension Reform: Toward Gender Equity

A number of reform measures address gender equity.[21] Beginning July 1, 2009, to increase a woman's pension, the government will provide a woman aged 65 or older with a bond equal to 18 monthly contributions based on the minimum wage, for each child she had. The bond covers the period of time from the child's birth up to the woman's 65th birthday. The rate of return will be based on the average annual rate (nominal) for Fund C less administrative fees for that time period. Both biological and adoptive mothers may receive the bond. The bond may be redeemed after the woman's 65th birthday and is combined with her retirement pension at that time.

Women who are eligible for this bond include those who have contributed to an individual account at least once during their working lives, those who receive the basic solidarity pension, and those who receive a survivor pension from either the individual account system or the public pension system. Women who retired before July 1, 2009, are not eligible for the bond.

Another measure to increase a woman's pension is related to premiums for survivors and disability insurance. An insurance company must calculate these premiums based on gender. Since women generally have lower incidences of survivors and disability claims, their rates are expected to be lower in most cases. The company will continue to charge the same premium for men and women, but refund to each woman the difference between the rate that she would have received and the rate for a man. That refund will be deposited directly into a woman's individual account and she will have a higher pension as a result.

Other provisions of the new law provide more gender equity:

- Widowers can become eligible for a survivor pension. (Previously, only disabled widowers were eligible.)
- In case of divorce or marriage annulment, the assets in an individual retirement account can be divided evenly between the ex-spouses, beginning October 1, 2008. Each ex-spouse can only receive 50 percent of the amount that had been accumulated during the marriage.[22]
- A worker is allowed to contribute to another person's individual account. The contribution must be at least based on the minimum salary.
- Women and men must be covered for survivors and disability insurance up to age 65. (Previously, women were covered up to age 60 and men up to age 65.)
- Beginning January 1, 2011, wages for domestic workers must be no less than the minimum wage for a full week of work or a percentage of the minimum wage for part-time work.[23] This will increase domestic workers' earnings and could result in a higher pension for these workers.

Policy Challenges: AFP Fees, Competition, and Profits

AFPs are a major focus of the pension reform. Since there has been little competition among the AFPs, the administrative fees they charge account holders are high, resulting in profits that are much larger than other sectors of Chile's financial services industry. Account holders have had lower net rates of return (and smaller pensions) in part because AFPs have charged high administrative fees.

Administrative Fees

Administrative fees charged to account holders have been high according to international standards. AFPs have been allowed to charge two types of administrative fees each time a worker contributes to an individual account: a percentage of earnings and a fixed fee. Between 1981 and 1987, the AFPs were also permitted to charge fees on the account balance. According to Mesa Lago and Arenas de Mesa (2006), the average cost of the combined fees to account holders increased by 4.8 percent between 1982 and 2003. In September 2008, the five existing AFPs charged an average of 1.71 percent of earnings and two out of the five AFPs charged fixed monthly fees: 320 pesos (US$0.61) and 690 pesos (US$1.31) (SUPEN 2007–2008).

Account holders only pay an administrative fee when they contribute to their account. In effect, the contributors are subsidizing the noncontributors. According to the Association of AFPs (2008a), by the end of 2007, some 3.5 million mandatory individual accounts (about 40 percent of all mandatory accounts) were subsidized. This means that about 40 percent of affiliates with mandatory accounts were noncontributors and were not paying any administrative fees.

Even though most AFPs had eliminated the fixed fee by the middle of 2008, they raised their percentage of earnings fees. In April 2006, when five of the six AFPs charged a fixed fee, they charged an average 1.60 percent of earnings fee. As of April 2008, when only two AFPs had fixed fees, the average percentage of earnings fees was 1.67 percent (SAFP 2005–2008).

Fixed fees are proportionately higher for low-wage earners than for high-wage earners. For example, between 1981 and 2004, a low-income affiliate with about US$315 in an individual account had an average real net rate of return of 6.2 percent per year compared with 8.2 percent per year for a higher income affiliate with a US$950 account balance (Mesa Lago and Arenas de Mesa 2006). The higher cost of the fixed fees on lower earners could have created a disincentive to participate in the individual account system (Gill, Packard, and Yermo 2005).

A 2005 SAFP study (Castro 2005a) calculated the effect of the fixed fee on a worker's final account balance just before retirement: a 1 percent reduction in the fixed fee would result in a 9 percent increase over the worker's lifetime for lower earners and a 3 percent increase for an average earner. The effect on higher earners is even lower. By completely eliminating the fixed fees, a minimum wage worker's account balance would increase by 4 percent each time he or she contributed and an average earner's balance would increase by 1.5 percent. The fixed fee represented about 9 percent of AFP earnings.

The 2005 study also concluded that eliminating the fixed fee would encourage competition among the AFPs while reducing AFP profits. The study predicted that AFPs would probably raise their percentage of earnings fees by 20 percentage points and would probably offer fewer products for the lower earner. If workers in general paid no fixed fee, their pensions could increase by between 15 percent and 20 percent. As a result, by 2024 the government would pay about 5.5 percent less for the guaranteed minimum benefit because workers' pensions would be higher.

The International Association of Pension Fund Management Companies Supervision Bodies (*Asociación Internacional de Organismos de Supervisión de Administradoras de Fondos de Pensiones* or AIOS) compared administrative fees as a percentage of the contribution to an individual account (mandatory contribution plus administrative fees) in 10 Latin American countries as of June 2007. In some countries both the employer and the employee are required to make monthly contributions. Table 3 shows that the fees ranged from 4.8 percent of the contribution in Bolivia to 17.8 percent in Argentina and the fees in Chile represented 14.6 percent of the contribution (AIOS 2007).

Competition among the AFPs

Since there has been little competition among the five existing AFPs, little incentive exists for them to lower their fees. According to the Marcel Commission, competition is weak because:

- Most workers do not compare administrative fees before choosing an AFP.

Table 3. Fees and Contributions in Individual Accounts in Latin American Countries as of June 2007 (Percent)

Country	Admin fee[a]	Mandatory contribution[a]	Fees as a percentage of contributions
Argentina	1.00	4.61	17.8
Bolivia[c]	0.50	10.00	4.8
Chile	1.71	10.00	14.6
Colombia[d]	1.58	11.00	12.6
Costa Rica	0.29	3.96	6.7
Dom Rep	0.60	7.40	7.5
El Salvador	1.40	10.00	12.3
México	1.02	7.48	12.0
Peru	1.81	10.00	15.3
Uruguay[e]	1.79	12.22	12.8

Source: AIOS 2007.

Note: AIOS = Asociación Internacional de Organ ismos de Supervisión de Administradoras de Fondos de Pensiones.

a. As a percentage of the worker's salary.

b. The employee's contribution as a percentage of salary, except in Colombia, Dominican Republic, El Salvador and Mexico where the figure also includes the employer's contribution as a percentage of covered payroll.

c. A fee for administering the investment portfolio is also charged.

d. Fees are also charged for transferring, exiting, and making voluntary contributions.

e. A custody fee on the account balance is also charged.

- AFPs are required to charge all their members the same fees. Since the profit margins are higher for higher earners, AFPs have tended to target higher earners. AFPs did not have to lower their fees since they often used gifts and other incentives to lure new members.
- Regulatory barriers have made it hard for new companies to enter the pension market. Banks are specifically prohibited from setting up an AFP.

When the system of individual accounts was implemented in 1981, there were 12 AFPs and by 1994, there were 21. In 2008 there are five AFPs. The decline in the number of AFPs was due to mergers and closures. Also, between 1982 and 2007, the percentage of affiliates in the largest three AFPs grew from 64 percent to nearly 80 percent (Mesa Lago and Arenas de Mesa 2006; SAFP 2005–2008).

AFP Profits

Pension fund industry profits have been much higher than other related industries. Between 1991 and 2004, AFPs earned an average of 27 percent on assets compared with an average of 15.7 percent during the same period for the Chilean financial services industry. In 2005, administrative fees represented 91 percent of an AFP's income and the yield on investments from the reserve fund was about 8 percent. AFP expenses for the same year included the cost of survivors and disability insurance (51 percent), administrative expenses (30 percent) and sales force salaries (11 percent) (Marcel Commission 2006).

Pension Reform: AFP Fees, Competition, and Profits

To increase competition among AFPs and lower costs to account holders, Law 20.255:

- Eliminates the monthly fixed administrative fees that most AFPs charge their account holders.
- Assigns all new labor force entrants to an AFP with the lowest fees. The AFP would have to maintain that fee for 24 months and offer the same low-rate fee structure to all its account holders.
- Eliminates the rate-of-return fluctuation fund and distributes the monies to AFP members beginning October 1, 2008. Previously, if a particular AFP fund's (Funds A through E) performance exceeded the average by a given percentage, it had to place the excess in a rate-of-return fluctuation fund. If any AFP fund's performance fell below the average, it had to make up the difference from both its excess rate-of-return and reserve funds.
- Improves AFP efficiency by allowing them to contract out certain functions such as administering the individual accounts and receiving applications for pensions and submitting them to the appropriate AFPs.
- Allows insurance companies to set up AFPs as a subsidiary. Congress rejected the provision that allows banks to set up an AFP as a subsidiary.

A number of provisions of the new law aim to improve the system's rate of return. A 1 percent increase in the rate of return during a person's working life can increase a pension by about 20 percent. The law gradually increases the limit on foreign investments to 80 percent of assets (from the current 45 percent) and intends to make the structure of all investment limits more flexible. For advice on investment of assets, a technical investment council will be created. The council will have five members: one designated by the president, another by the Central Bank, one by the AFPs, and two nominated by the deans of economic departments in accredited Chilean universities. In addition, each AFP must set up a technical investment committee that establishes investment policies for each type of fund.

Policy Challenge: Premiums for Survivors and Disability Insurance

Premiums for survivors and disability insurance have increased recently, another cost for the worker. Each AFP contracts with an insurance company to provide survivors and disability insurance for its account holders. The amount of the premium has varied from one AFP to another and the average premium among all the AFPs has fluctuated over time. Between 1994 and 2003, the average premium rose from 0.86 percent to 1.14 percent of a worker's earnings (Castro 2005b). At the end of 2006, the average cost was 0.73 percent of a worker's earnings and by September 2008, that figure had risen to 0.99 percent (SUPEN 2007–2008).

Pension Reform: Survivors and Disability Insurance

Law 20.255 makes a number of changes to survivors and disability insurance:

- All AFPs must select an insurance company for survivors and disability insurance through a bidding process.
- Premiums will be the same for all account holders.
- Beginning July 1, 2009, employers must pay the cost of survivors and disability insurance for their employees. Until June 2011, employers with fewer than 100 employees will be exempt.

The disability determination process has also been changed. While the definitions of total and partial disability remain the same (according to the percentage loss of earning capacity), a worker will no longer have a 3-year waiting period to be assessed as permanently totally disabled. Only partial disability will require a final assessment after 3 years. In addition, a worker will be able to select his or her own doctor for a medical evaluation, paid for by the worker. Otherwise the Medical Commission will pay for an evaluation performed by the doctor that it selects (Asociación AFP 2008b).

Policy Challenge: Voluntary Retirement Savings

Workers have not saved enough for retirement through additional voluntary contributions. Since August 1987, they have been permitted to set up separate voluntary retirement savings accounts. A 2002 law provides tax incentives for voluntary retirement savings and encourages competition by allowing other types of institutions—including banks, brokerage houses, insurance companies, and mutual funds—to offer voluntary retirement savings accounts (Kritzer 2001/2002). However, the tax incentives have benefited mainly higher income workers (Berstein, Larrain, and Pino 2006). At the end of 2006, 20 percent of the close to 7.7 million AFP members had voluntary retirement savings accounts. Nonetheless, 46 percent of these accounts had a zero balance (SAFP 2005–2008).

Pension Reform: Voluntary Retirement Savings

The reform includes a provision to encourage more voluntary retirement savings. At present, few Chilean companies offer occupational pension plans. One reform measure creates employer-sponsored voluntary pension plans, known as Ahorro Previsional Voluntario Colectivo (APVC), which target the middle class. APVC supplements the existing voluntary retirement savings accounts beginning in October 2008. Both employers and employees can contribute to an APVC. Workers enrolled in an APVC plan who contribute up to 1.5 million pesos (US$2,913) a year to a voluntary account (and regularly contribute to a mandatory retirement account) will be eligible for an annual government subsidy of 15 percent of the amount that the worker has voluntarily saved for retirement.[24]

Policy Challenge: Financial Literacy

Workers on the whole do not understand the system of individual accounts, according to the results of the EPS. The Marcel Commission acknowledged that the system is difficult to comprehend.

According to the EPS for 2004, most of those surveyed did not know how their pensions were calculated, did not understand the relationship between contributions to an individual account and their pensions, and were not familiar with the basic facts about the guaranteed minimum pension and its requirements. EPS findings include:

- Fewer than 50 percent of those surveyed reported that they were aware of the required monthly contribution; only about 30 percent of respondents provided accurate answers. About 2 percent were familiar with either the fixed or percentage administrative fee; none were familiar with both types of fees.
- Of the 50 percent who reported that they were aware of how much they had in their individual account, the amount that two-thirds of them reported was more than 20 percent different from the actual amount.
- Only about 8 percent of those surveyed knew how pensions are calculated.
- Even though half of them stated that they knew about the multifunds, only 20 percent knew how many fund options exist.
- Those with less education and less money are less likely to have knowledge about the system.
- The majority of those surveyed knew the correct normal retirement age.
- About two-thirds of the pensioners surveyed were aware of what kind of benefit they receive, but the amount they reported receiving ranged from 20 percent less to 20 percent more than the actual benefit amount (Bravo 2006; Arenas de Mesa and others 2006).

Pension Reform: Financial Education

To improve financial literacy in Chile, the new law establishes a social security education fund, financed by contributions from the state and private donations to develop a financial education program through a competitive process. The fund was set up in July 2008 and is supervised by the ministry of labor and undersecretary of social security. Also, the government will establish an accreditation system for pension advisors to create a network of professional advisors that provide professional and independent financial advice to account holders. These professional advisors will be permitted to charge a fee of 2 percent of the worker's individual account balance, up to a maximum of 60 UF (US$ 2,427) (Asociación AFP 2008a).

Pension Reform: New Government Agencies

The reform creates a new organizational structure. On July 4, 2008, the Superintendent of Pensions (SUPEN) replaced the Superintendent of Pension Fund Management Companies (SAFP) (SUPEN 2008). SUPEN supervises both the mandatory and voluntary individual account systems and oversees the Social Security Institute (IPS), another new agency responsible for the new solidarity pillar as well as the public PAYG pension system. The IPS will set up local offices around the country to provide more access and better service to the insured.

Every 5 years SUPEN and the ministry of finance's budget director will be responsible for an actuarial study that evaluates the effect of demographic and financial changes on the replacement rates for the individual account system.

Projected Cost of the Reform

The Marcel Commission estimated the annual cost of the new solidarity pillar at 2.5 percent of GDP and its recommended changes to the contributory pillar at about 2.9 percent of GDP. By 2025, these combined annual costs could equal about 1.3 percent of GDP more than the cost of operating the current system including means-tested benefits and the obligations of the PAYG public system (benefits to current pensioners plus the recognition bonds). To provide greater financial stability for future social program spending, the government set up a pension reserve fund in 2006, financed in part from the budget surplus and the revenues from the sale of copper[25] (SSA 2006–2008).

Conclusion

In 1981, Chile was the first country to switch from a public PAYG pension system to individual accounts.

Over the years, the system has undergone some major changes, including broadening the allowable investments and introducing a choice of several types of pension funds with varying degrees of risk levels. Twenty-six years later, the country's new pension reform law provides the most comprehensive overhaul of the individual account system since its inception. The International Monetary Fund supports these changes because they strive to retain the basic features of the individual account system and, at the same time, address its major shortcomings. The reform expands coverage and creates a basic benefit for many Chileans who would not otherwise qualify for a pension. Other measures will improve gender equity, encourage competition in the pension fund industry, and lower costs to help raise the net rate of return for account holders; thus, providing higher pensions.

Since the 1990s, 10 other Latin American countries have adopted some form of an individual account system either to replace or supplement their PAYG systems. As other capitalization systems in the region have matured, they too have begun expanding allowable AFP investments and a few have increased the number of fund choices. Just as Chile has passed a major overhaul of its individual account system, other countries are beginning to examine the shortcomings of their systems. Peru has set up a pension commission and Uruguay has created a "social security dialogue." Mexico introduced multifunds in March 2008 and Colombia will follow suit. Both Argentina and Peru have passed laws that allow workers to switch back to the public system.

Chile's next generation pension reform could influence changes in a number of these Latin American countries. Law 20.255 addresses many of the same issues that other systems are confronting and can serve as a frame of reference for these other countries. The individual account systems in each of these countries are a work in progress.

References

Arenas de Mesa, Alberto & others. (2006). *The Chilean pension reform turns 25: Lessons from the social protection survey*. Pension Research Council

Working Paper No. 2006-9, Philadelphia, PA: The Wharton School, University of Pennsylvania.

Asociación AFP. (2004a). Nuevo sistema previsional está pagando 530 mil pensiones. Serie de estudios Número 46.

———. (2004b). Sistemas de consulta y ofertas de montos de pensiones: Afiliados de AFP deberán aceptar o rechazar formar parte del listo público para pensionarse. Serie de estudios Número 44.

———. (2006). Nuevo dictamen de la superintendencia de AFP: Mujeres divorciadas y anuladas no tienen derecho a pensión de viudez. Serie de estudios Número 55.

———. (2008a). AFP han impulsado el ahorro individual y hoy administran 11.6 millones de cuentas. Serie de estudios Número 63.

———. (2008b). Comunica AFP. Número 98.

———. (2008c). Multifondos resultados y tendencias. Multifondos Boletín Número 20.

———. (2008d). Retiro programado y renta vitalicia son modalidades complementarias. Serie de estudios Número 65.

[AIOS] Asociación Internacional de Organismos de Supervisión de Fondos de Pensiones. (2007). Boletín Estadístico Número 18.

Berstein, Solange, Guillermo Larrain & Francisco Pino. (2006). Chilean pension reform: Coverage facts and policy alternatives. *Journal of the Latin American and Caribbean Economic Association, 6(2)*, 227–279.

Berstein, Solange & Rómulo Chumacero. (2003). *Quantifying the costs of investment limits for Chilean pension funds*. The Pensions Institute Discussion Paper No. PI-0403, London: Cass Business School.

Bertranou, Fabio M. & Javiera Vásquez. (2007). Trabajadores independientes y cobertura de seguridad social en Chile. Oficina Internacional del Trabajo. (24 de agosto).

Bravo, David, (2006). The Chilean pension reform turns 25:Lessons from the social protection survey. Paper pre-sented at the 2006 Atlanta Federal Reserve Conference.

Bravo, David & others. (2008). Encuesta de protección social 2006: Presentación general y principales resultados. (Enero).

Castro, Rubén. (2005a). Efectos de largo plazo de la comisión fija en el sistema chileno de AFP. Serie Documentos de Trabajo, Número 9, Superintendencia de Administradoras de Fondos de Pensiones.

———. (2005b). Seguro de invalidez y sobreviviencia: Qué es y qué le está pasando. Serie Documentos de Trabajo, Número 5, Superintendencia de Administradoras de Fondos de Pensiones.

[Marcel Commission] Consejo Asesor Presidencial para la Reforma Previsional. (2006). El derecho a una vida digna en la vejez: Hacia un contrato social con la previsión en Chile. *http://www.consejorefor maprevisional.cl/view/* presentacion.asp.

[Law 3500] Decreto Ley Número 3500 de 1980. (2007). Actualizado a julio de.

[Law 20.25 5] Decreto Ley Número 20.255. el 11 de marzo de. (2008).

Gallardo, Eduardo. Chile's model pension system reformed. Miami Herald. March 17, 2008, http://www.miamiherald .com/.

Gill, Indermit S., Truman Packard & Juan Yermo. (2005). *Keeping the promise of social security in Latin America*. Washington, DC: The World Bank.

[ISSA] International Social Security Association. (2008). *Social Security worldwide*. http://www-ssw.issa.int/ sswlp2/engl/page1 .htm.

James, Estelle & Augusto Iglesias. (2007). *Disability insurance with prefunding and private participation: The Chilean model*. Michigan Retirement Research Center, Policy Brief Number 4, Ann Arbor, MI: University of Michigan.

James, Estelle, Guillermo Martinez & Augusto Iglesias. (2006). The payout stage in Chile: Who annuitizes and why? *Journal of Pension Economics and Finance*, *5(2)*, 121–1 54.

Kritzer, Barbara. (2001/2002). Recent changes to the Chilean system of individual accounts. *Social Security Bulletin*, *64(4)*, 67–71.

Mesa Lago, Carmelo & Alberto Arenas de Mesa. (2006). The structural pension reform in Chile: Effects, comparisons and other Latin American reforms, and lessons. *Oxford Review of Economic Policy*, *22(1)*, 149–167.

[Mideplan] Ministerio de Planificación. (2007). Encuesta CASEN evidencia importantes cambios en las familias chilenas. http://www.mideplan.cl.

Ministerio del Trabajo y Previsión Social. (2008). Reforma previsional Chile valora tu vida, manual informativo. *http://www.reformaprevisional.cl /reforma_previsional/* documentos/Manual%20Informativo%20Reforma%20 Previsional.pdf.

Perry, Guillermo E. & others. (2007). *Informality exit and exclusion*. Washington, DC: The World Bank, Latin American and Caribbean Studies.

San Juan, Patricia. 2nd update: Chile '07 fiscal surplus hits record 8.7 percent of GDP. Dow Jones International News, January 30, 2008.

[SAFP] Superintendencia de Administradora de Fondos de Pensiones. (2005–2008). Boletín Estadístico.

———. (2007). El sistema chileno. 6ª Edición. Santiago, Chile.

[SUPEN] Superintendencia de Pensiones. (2007–2008). Centro de Estadísticas. Sistema de Pensiones. *http://www .safp.cl/safpstats/ stats/.sc.php?_cid=41.*

———. (2008). Comunicado de prensa. el 4 de julio de 2008.

Umar, Tarik. (2007). Americas: Breaking barriers. *Harvard International Review, 28(4).*

[SSA] Social Security Administration. (2006–2008). International Update. http://www.ssa.gov/policy.

———. (2008). *Social Security programs throughout the world: The Americas*, 2007. Washington, DC: Office of Retirement and Disability Policy, Office of Research, Evaluation, and Statistics.

Williamson, John. (2005). An update on Chile's experience with partial privatization and individual accounts. AARP Public Policy Institute. (December). http://assets.aarp.org/ rgcenter/econ/2005_1 9_chile.pdf.

End Notes

[1] Unidad de Fomento (UF) is a monetary unit adjusted daily to reflect changes in the consumer price index. In Chile, most financial contracts, including pensions, are denominated in UFs. On September 4, 2008, one UF equaled 20,820.35 pesos (US$40) (http://www.uf.cl/).

[2] For a more extensive comparison of the different options at retirement, see Asociación AFP 2008d.

[3] This fourth option was created by the 2004 Annuities Law.

[4] As of April 2008, the monthly MPG for retirees under age 70 was 96,390.73 pesos (US$187), between ages 70 and 75 was 105,395.85 pesos (US$204) and 75 or older, 112,453.82 pesos (US$218). At the same time, the minimum monthly wage was 144,000 pesos (US$330) (SAFP 2005–2008).

[5] To qualify for the MPG, a disabled worker must have at least 2 years of contributions in the 5 years before the onset of the disability or be making contributions at the onset of the disability (SSA 2008).

[6] Workers compensation is a separate program.

[7] When the provisions of the new law relating to disability are implemented, the disability determination process will be modified (see section "Pension Reform: Survivors and Disability Insurance.")

[8] An immediate annuity, a deferred annuity, and an immediate annuity with programmed withdrawals.

[9] The minimum and maximum rate of return has been a requirement since the inception of the program. The multi- fund law expanded the requirement so that each type of fund has its own minimum and maximum rates of return.

[10] The Association of AFPs publishes a series entitled, "Multifonds, Resultados y Tendencias" every 3 months that monitors the performance of the multifunds. The most recent issue is March 2008 (Asociación AFP 2008c).

[11] In the 1980s a major portion of AFPs assets under management were in government bonds. At that time, the government paid high interest rates to the AFPs for these bonds, especially

during the first few years after the individual account system was implemented. Several analysts also consider these high interest rates a result of the government fiscal crisis in 1982 that raised the bonds' risk level (Williamson 2005).

[12] For more information on SCOMP, see Asociación AFP 2004b.

[13] The President's Pension Advisory Commission was appointed by President Bachelet in March 2006 to evaluate the individual accounts system. The Commission, also known as the Marcel Commission (Mario Marcel, the former budget director, led the Commission), presented their report to the President in July 2006. It contained a comprehensive evaluation of the system as well as 70 reform proposals (Marcel Commission 2006; SSA 2006–2008).

[14] The sources for the details of law 20.255 are Ministerio del Trabajo y Prevision Social 2008 and DL 20.255, unless otherwise noted.

[15] For a detailed study on social security coverage of the self-employed, see Bertranou and Vásquez 2007.

[16] The 2002 survey was called the History of Labor and Social Security Survey. After the 2004 EPS was conducted, to simply the terminology, researchers began to refer to the 2002 survey as an EPS as well. The EPS was conducted for 2006 and is scheduled for 2008. It is expected every two years after that, subject to funding availability (Bravo 2008; Arenas de Mesa and others 2006; Berstein, Larrain, and Pino 2006). For more information on the EPS, go to http:// www.proteccionsocial.cl/noticias.asp

[17] For an extensive study on the informal sector in Chile and other countries in Latin America, see Perry and others 2007.

[18] The MPG is equal to about 25 percent of average wage for retirees younger than age 70. The MPG for those aged 70 to 74 is about 27 percent and 29 percent for those aged 75 or older (James and Iglesias 2007).

[19] About two-thirds of old-age pensioners have annuitized—most of them have retired early. Close to two-thirds of disability pensioners have programmed withdrawals (James, Martinez, and Iglesias 2006).

[20] Recognition bonds are calculated using wages paid between 1976 and 1980. In Chile, during this time period, there were high rates of unemployment. As a result, those without a job at the time would not be eligible for the recognition bond (Berstein, Larrain, and Pino 2006).

[21] The Marcel Commission proposal to raise the retirement age for women from age 60 to age 65 was not included in the President's pension reform bill.

[22] Divorce was legalized in Chile in 2004. A 2005 ruling stated that ex-wives (as a result of divorce or annulment) are not entitled to a widow's pension (Asociación AFP 2006).

[23] This change will be phased in—from 83 percent of the minimum wage beginning January 1, 2009 to 92 percent of the minimum wage a year later.

[24] Up to a ceiling of 217,000 pesos (US$422) as of August 2008.

[25] The Pension Reserve Fund has assets of more than US$1.1 billion (Gallardo 2008). By the end of 2007, the budget surplus reached about US$16.3 billion, 8.7 percent of the country's GDP (San Juan 2008).

In: International Social Security: Agreements... ISBN: 978-1-61761-430-9
Editors: Nicole E. Pampino

Chapter 5

KIWISAVER: NEW ZEALAND'S NEW SUBSIDIZED RETIREMENT SAVINGS PLANS

Barbara E. Kritzer

INTRODUCTION

Since July 1, 2007, New Zealanders have had a new option for their retirement savings—KiwiSaver—a type of subsidized, defined contribution retirement savings plan offered by private-sector providers. New labor force entrants in permanent positions who are aged 18 or older are automatically enrolled in a KiwiSaver plan, but are able to opt out of the plan if they wish. Also, all individuals younger than age 65, including anyone not in the labor force, are permitted to set up a KiwiSaver account.

A law passed in September 2006 created the KiwiSaver to encourage New Zealanders to save more for retirement and to supplement the New Zealand Superannuation (NZS) benefit, a flat-rate universal old-age pension. Although lower earners mainly rely on NZS benefits for their retirement income, middle and higher earners must supplement this benefit to maintain their preretirement standard of living. Workers may also purchase supplementary retirement plans, called superannuation plans either through their employers or directly from an insurance or other financial services company.[1] The New Zealand government introduced the KiwiSaver, in part, because by the end of 2005, less than 30 percent of the active labor force was covered by some type of superannuation plan.

This note provides a brief description of the New Zealand public pension system and its sources of funding, statistics on the country's savings rates before the KiwiSaver law was passed, and a detailed description of KiwiS aver.

New Zealand's Public Pension

New Zealand Superannuation is the flat-rate public pension available to all New Zealand residents aged 65 or older who have lived in the country for 10 years since age 20, or for 5 years since age 50 (SSA 2007). NZS benefit amounts depend on marital status and living arrangements and are taxed as income. Each year benefit amounts for a married or civil union couple are adjusted for inflation and then adjusted to fall between 65.0 percent and 72.5 percent of the country's net average wage.[2] The NZS retirement benefit for other categories is computed as a percentage of the benefit amount for married couples and civil unions: single persons living alone receive 65 percent of the benefit, and single persons living with others receive 60 percent. NZS benefits are adjusted according to changes in the consumer price index (Toder and Khitatrakun 2006). NZS is the government's largest single budget item with a current net cost of 3.4 percent of gross domestic product (GDP), which is expected to rise to 6.9 percent of GDP by 2050 with the aging of the population (NZSF 2006).

Although NZS currently is funded by general revenues, as the population ages this program will need an additional source of funding to meet benefit payment projections. The New Zealand Superannuation Act 2001 created a separate investment fund called the New Zealand Superannuation Fund (NZSF, or the Fund) to partially finance the projected rise in costs of New Zealand Superannuation benefits as the country's population ages. From 1970 through 2005, while the overall population grew by 44 percent, the number of people aged 65 or older doubled. In 2006, the number of people aged 65 or older represented 12 percent of the population and is expected to reach 26 percent by 2051 (Statistics 2006). According to the National Population Projections, the ratio of the working-age population (aged 16–64) to the population aged 65 or older was 5.5 to 1.0 in 2004. This figure is expected to drop to 3.0 to 1.0 in 2028 and to 2.2 to 1.0 by 2051 (Statistics 2004).

The government expects to finance the NZSF from general revenues with an average contribution of NZ$1.95 billion (US$1.6 billion) a year until about 2027.[3] In September 2003, the government made the first payment to the NZSF of NZ$2.4 billion (US$ 1.9 billion). By October 30, 2007, its assets totaled NZ$14 billion (US$ 11.3 billion), and the average nominal rate of return since 2003 was 14.29 percent.

By law, the government may not withdraw any capital from the Fund before July 1, 2020. The New Zealand Treasury estimates that by about 2028, when the ratio of the working-age population to the population aged 65 or older falls to about 3 to 1, the government will stop contributing to the NZSF and begin taking money out of the Fund to cover about 15 percent of the net yearly superannuation costs from 2055 through 2075.[4] The Fund is expected to continue growing over time because the capital withdrawals are projected to be less than the Fund's income (NZSF 2006 and 2007; MSD 2007; Treasury 2006).

The Fund operates "at arms length" from the government. The Guardians of New Zealand Superannuation, a separate government organization, manages and administers the Fund's assets. The Board, which oversees the Guardians, is made up of five to seven members who are recommended by the Minister of Finance and appointed by the Governor General. A formal review of the Guardians' performance will be conducted about every 5 years by an independent agent appointed by the Minister of Finance (NZSF 2006).[5]

Saving for Retirement

KiwiSaver was introduced to help New Zealanders save more for retirement. In March 2007, Finance Minister Michael Cullen stated that New Zealanders have one of the lowest household savings rates among the developed countries. Cullen (2007a) cited the New Zealand Reserve Bank estimates of current household savings rate at negative 17.5 percent. A March 2007 New Zealand Treasury study concluded that about 20 percent of the population aged 45–64 needs to save more for retirement, including about 9 percent of individuals and 13 percent of couples aged 55–65 (Hosking 2007).[6]

A 2003 report from a panel of experts found that economic well-being in retirement may be substantially different for the future cohort of retirees, compared with current retirees.[7] The report concluded that a large percentage of current retirees are able to maintain their standard of living through a variety of sources: NZS, private savings, and mortgage-free home ownership. The report also found that although those nearing retirement should be able to meet their needs, younger workers may have lower standards of living in retirement because of high levels of debt, student loans, child-bearing at later ages, and potentially fewer mortgage-free homes (IBIS 2004).

Participation in supplementary retirement plans has been relatively low. In New Zealand, voluntary supplementary retirement plans (called superannuation plans) are available through employers or directly from an insurance or other financial services company. At the end of 2005, more than 600,000 individuals were enrolled in some type of superannuation plan with a total of NZ$18.2 billion (US$14.6 billion) in assets. Half of these individuals (about 13 percent of the labor force) were enrolled in employer-sponsored retirement superannuation plans with a total of NZ$11.5 billion (US$9.2 billion) in assets (MED 2006).[8] According to the 2001 Household Savings Survey, less than 20 percent of those who earned between NZ$15,000 and NZ$50,000 (US$12,000 and US$40,000) per year were enrolled in some type of superannuation plan. The government is targeting this group of earners with KiwiSaver (Cullen 2007b).

KiwiSaver

KiwiSaver is a new type of subsidized, defined contribution retirement savings plan created to supplement NZS and help increase an individual's retirement income.[9]

Eligibility

Beginning July 1, 2007, new permanent workers aged 18–65 are automatically enrolled in a workplace KiwiSaver plan, but have from the second to the eighth week of their employment to opt out of the plan.[10] Anyone younger than age 65, including the self-employed and anyone not in the labor force, may choose to set up a KiwiSaver account with any provider. Workers who are automatically enrolled in a KiwiSaver plan may choose to move their account to another provider at any time. Those aged 65 or older may continue to contribute to their KiwiS aver account as long as they joined a plan before age 65. Although individuals are permitted only one KiwiSaver account, workers with multiple jobs may contribute to their account from each of their current jobs.

Individuals who are younger than age 65 and either citizens of New Zealand or entitled to stay in New Zealand indefinitely are permitted to have a KiwiSaver account as long as they reside in the country. New Zealand government employees working outside of the country may also opt into a KiwiSaver plan.

CONTRIBUTIONS AND GOVERNMENT SUBSIDIES

Workers may select a monthly contribution rate of either 4 percent or 8 percent of gross earnings; those who do not choose either rate will automatically be assigned a 4 percent contribution rate. Workers may increase their contribution up to the 8 percent rate at any time. KiwiSaver account holders who contribute to their account will receive a tax credit of up to NZ$20 (US$16) a week and NZ$1,040 (US$836) a year that will be deposited directly into their KiwiS aver account.

Until April 1, 2008, employers had the option of paying part or all of an employee's KiwiS aver contribution. The employer's contribution of up to 4 percent of the employee's gross earnings was tax-exempt to the employer.[11] Because this is not a matching contribution, the total employer/employee contribution was either 4 percent or 8 percent.

Beginning April 1, 2008, all employers are required to contribute to an employee's KiwiS aver account: starting with 1 percent of the employee's gross salary in 2008 and adding 1 percent each year until the mandatory employer contribution reaches 4 percent of gross salary by April 1, 2011. Employers receive a tax credit of up to NZ $20 (US$16) per week per employee (Cullen 2007).

Another arrangement is possible between April 2008 and March 2011. If both the employer and the employee agree, they are permitted to divide the employee's contribution: in 2008, each would contribute 2 percent of the employee's gross earnings; by 2010, each would contribute 3 percent; and by 2011, they both would contribute 4 percent.[12]

Employers must withhold contributions beginning with a new employee's first paycheck, unless the employee opts out of the program (between the second and eighth week of employment). Those who opt out of the program will receive a refund of their contributions. The government tax authority,

Inland Revenue, collects the contributions from employers and distributes them to the employees' KiwiSaver plans.

The New Zealand government provides two other subsidies (in addition to the tax credit): a one-time tax-free payment of NZ$1,000 (US$804) to each KiwiS aver account after the individual plan receives the first contribution to that account; and, a NZ$40 (US$32) annual fee subsidy to each account holder to defray administrative costs. The fee subsidy is payable up to age 65, or 5 years after a worker older than age 60 first sets up a KiwiSaver account. The government has not set a limit on how much providers may charge account holders for administrative fees.

"Contribution Holiday" and Early Withdrawals

After the first 12 months of membership, automatically enrolled workers may take a "contribution holiday" for a minimum of 3 months, up to 5 years at a time for any reason. However, workers with a serious illness or experiencing a financial hardship may take the "contribution holiday" before the end of the first year of membership. Details of the "contribution holiday" provision for those who contract directly with a plan (the self-employed, those who are not in the labor force, and workers younger than age 65 who choose a KiwiSaver plan that is not sponsored by their employer) are dependent on the particular plan provider. Also, some plans and mortgage providers may allow account holders to divert up to one-half of their contribution to pay for a mortgage after contributing to a KiwiSaver account for 12 months.

After the opt-out period expires, KiwiSaver participants may withdraw all of their funds at age 65 or 5 years after they opened their account, whichever is later, and at any time in the event of serious illness.[13] Participants may withdraw all of their contributions and any vested employer contributions if they:

- face significant financial hardship such as the member's or dependent's medical care, a dependent's education, or the member's inability to meet minimum living expenses according to normal community standards determined by law;
- leave the country permanently; or,
- make a down payment on the purchase of a first home after at least 3 years of saving in a KiwiSaver account. Beginning in 2011, the

government plans to provide an eligible first-time home buyer who has a KiwiSaver account (subject to income and housing cost limits) with a home ownership subsidy of NZ$1,000 (US$804) per year, up to a maximum of NZ$5,000 (US$4,018) per person (Treasury 2007).

PROVIDERS

Workers who have been automatically enrolled and do not choose a registered provider are assigned to a default provider.[14] The Ministry of Economic Development approves all KiwiS aver providers including a limited number of default providers selected through a tender process.[15] It is also responsible for supervising KiwiSaver plans, issuing provider and plan regulations, and negotiating fees with the default providers. Although the default providers offer only plans with a conservative investment portfolio, other registered providers are permitted to provide a variety of investment portfolios such as conservative, balanced, or growth. KiwiSaver accounts are portable and members may change plans and investment risk portfolios at any time. The government provides no guarantees for the funds in KiwiSaver accounts.

Employers must provide access to a KiwiSaver plan to all employees although workers may choose any registered KiwiSaver plan. Employers may convert their existing employer-sponsored superannuation plan to a KiwiSaver; they may also request an exemption from the government from providing their employees with access to a KiwiSaver plan, if their registered superannuation plan meets certain criteria such as limiting employees' access to their retirement savings and requiring them to contribute at least 4 percent of earnings to their employer's superannuation plan.

FINANCIAL EDUCATION

The New Zealand Retirement Commission is charged with providing workplace financial education programs to help workers make informed decisions about establishing a KiwiSaver account. The Commission, established in 1993, has been conducting financial education programs around the country on a wide range of topics including saving, debt management, housing, and understanding net worth. Until now, workplace financial education focused solely on retirement seminars for workers nearing retirement. The new financial education program will help individuals assess whether or not KiwiSaver is appropriate for them (Feslier 2006). The Commission's public information Web site, http://www.sorted.org.nz, provides free financial education information including online tools to help workers make an informed decision about KiwiSaver (MSD 2007).[16]

Recent Tax Incentives for Retirement Savings

The original KiwiSaver bill submitted to Parliament in February 2006 did not contain any tax exemptions.[17] However, just before its passage by Parliament in August 2006, tax incentives for employer contributions to KiwiSaver plans were added to the bill. As a result, the Association of Superannuation Funds of New Zealand lobbied the government to extend the same tax breaks to these occupational pension plans so that KiwiSaver plans would not have what was perceived as an unfair advantage over superannuation plans. Thus, the December 2006 tax bill passed by Parliament contained a provision that allows the same tax breaks to superannuation plans with the same requirements as the KiwiSaver: fully portable, full vesting, and "lock-in until retirement." In May, Finance Minister Cullen announced in his "Budget 2007" speech some additional changes to KiwiS aver and qualified superannuation plans: a tax credit for employees and phased-in mandatory employer contributions. Legislation for the employee tax credit was enacted in May 2007 (Tax Policy 2007) and the provision for mandatory employer contributions was enacted in December 2007.

Take-up Rate

Before the tax incentives for workers were added to the KiwiSaver bill, the government had predicted that 345,000 workers would have a KiwiSaver account in the first year and by 2013, that figure would reach 700,000—about 25 percent of all eligible individuals. When the KiwiSaver law was passed (with tax incentives), the government estimated that 50 percent of those eligible would have a KiwiSaver account no later than 2017. Based on the later estimates, the government predicted that its annual expenditures on KiwiSaver could be close to NZ$2billion (US$1.6 billion) per year as early as 2012 (Cullen 2007b).

By the end of 2007, the take-up rate far exceeded government predictions—more than 300,000 workers were enrolled in a KiwiSaver plan.[18] According to the Retirement Commission's 2007 Review of Retirement Income Policy, based on the current rate of enrollment, the government incentives could be much more costly than the most recent estimates. The Commission urged Treasury to estimate the likely future costs of KiwiS aver to the government including the sustainability of the current incentives (Retirement Commission 2007c).

PROGRAM EVALUATION

Researchers have pointed out a number of unresolved issues concerning KiwiSaver, which include the following:

- The government could negotiate such low administrative fees with the default providers that smaller, nondefault providers might not be able to compete.
- Saving for retirement and saving for a first home could be conflicting goals that could undermine the retirement savings aspect of KiwiSaver.
- An individual may contribute for only 12 months to qualify for the government subsidy and then take a "contribution holiday." The potential for thousands of inactive accounts with very low balances could be very costly to administer.
- The choice between contribution rates of only 4 percent and 8 percent of salary can limit the amount an individual is able to contribute to an account. If there were more options, such as gradually increasing the rate from 4 percent to 8 percent of salary over a period of 4 years, a larger number of account holders might be able to afford to contribute more to their KiwiS aver account as their salaries rise.
- Many first-time home buyers would be excluded from a KiwiSaver housing subsidy because the limits on household income and the cost of the house are likely to be relatively low. (Because this aspect of KiwiS aver will not be introduced until 2011, the limits have yet to be established.)

- The KiwiSaver law does not address the issue of how to protect the value of the savings after withdrawal. A lump-sum withdrawal is permitted at retirement and there is no requirement to use these funds for retirement. Also, the law does not include measures to encourage the growth of the annuities market. Because only a few companies currently offer annuities, rates are not competitive and the types of annuities available are limited. (Toder and Khitatrakun 2006; St. John and Little- wood 2006a and 2006b).

The government is in the process of developing the KiwiS aver Evaluation Program to assess the strengths and weaknesses of KiwiSaver. The program could address some of the previously mentioned unresolved issues. Inland Revenue, Treasury, the Ministry of Economic Development, and the Ministry of Social Development are working on this policy initiative. The government intends to evaluate KiwiS aver from its inception to make program improvements quickly. Areas of study will include levels of participation, cost effectiveness, and public awareness of KiwiSaver. The New Zealand government hopes that the data they collect will help other countries that are considering automatic enrollment retirement savings programs (MSD 2007; Retirement Commission 2007a).

REFERENCES

Costo, Stephanie. (2006). Trends in retirement plan coverage over the last decade. *Monthly Labor Review, 129(2)*, 58–64.

Cullen, Michael. (2007a). "Reserve Bank highlights savings problem." Speech (March 8). http://www.beehive .govt.nz.

———. (2007b). "Government dealing with savings challenge." Speech (March 16). http://www.beehive.govt.nz.

———. (2007c). "Budget 2007." Speech (May 17). http:// www.beehive.govt.nz.

Feslier, David. (2006). *Financial education and financial literacy in New Zealand* (September). *http://www.oecd.org/dataoecd/15/53/ 374246 33.pdf.*

Hosking, Rob. (2007). Proof that Cullen's savings 'problem' is exaggerated. *National Business Review* (March 23). http://global.factiva.com.

[IBIS] International Benefits Information Service. (2004). *New Zealand:*

Private retirement savings working group (June).

Le, Trinh, Grant Scobie & John Gibson. (2007). *Are Kiwis saving enough for retirement? Preliminary evidence from SOFIE. New Zealand Treasury.* Paper prepared for the 8th Annual SuperFunds Summit, Wellington (March 15–16).

Littlewood, Michael. (2005). *"New Zealand: Prefunding Tier 1 pensions—lessons from New Zealand."* Second International Workshop on the Balance Sheet of Social Security Pensions. Tokyo, Japan (December 15).

[Labour]. *New Zealand Department of Labour. (2007). Older people in work: Key trends and patterns*, 1991–2005 (February).

New Zealand Government. (2007). KiwiSaver Web site. *http://www kiwisaver.govt.nz.*

[Tax Policy] New Zealand Inland Revenue Policy Advice Division. (2007). Urgent legislation enacted (May 22). http://www.taxpolicy.ird.govt.nz.

[MED] *New Zealand Ministry of Economic Development, Insurance and Superannuation Unit. (2006).* Report of the government actuary for the year ended 30 June.

[MSD] *New Zealand Ministry of Social Development*. (2007). Older people's policy office. Personal communication (February).

New Zealand Superannuation Act. (2001). Public Act 2001. No. 84. http://executive.govt.nz/MINISTER/cullen/ superannuation/super_act_ 2001 .pdf.

[NZSF] New Zealand Superannuation Fund. (2006). *Annual Report*. http://www.nzsuperfund.co.nz.

———. (2007). http://www.nzsuperfund.co.nz.

[Treasury] New Zealand Treasury. (2006). New Zealand Superannuation Fund contribution rate model: Half-year economic and fiscal update 2006 (December 19).

———. (2007). Budget 2007. Savers Fact Sheet (May). *http://www.treasury. govt.nz/budget/2007/kiwisaver/* pdfs/b07-ks-savers-fact-v2.pdf.

Retirement Commission. (2007a). Public information Web site. http://www.sorted.org.nz.

———. (2007b). Policy initiatives. http://www.retirement

———. (2007c). *2007 Review of Retirement Income Policy*. http://www.retirement Retirementjncome_Policy.pdf.

St. John, Susan. (2001). *New Zealand goes it alone in superannuation policy. Paper presented at the 9th Annual Colloquium of Superannuation Researchers*. University of New South Wales (July 9–10).

St. John, Susan, & Michael Littlewood. (2006a). *Submission on the KiwiSaver bill*. Paper presented at Parliament's Select Committee Hearing (May 3).

———. (2006b). *Does KiwiSaver improve the unique NewZealand mix of retirement policies*? Paper presented at the 14th Australian Colloquium of Superannuation Researchers: Choice of Retirement Funding, UNSW, Sydney (July 20–21).

[Statistics] Statistics New Zealand. (2004). National population projections (December). http://www.stats.govt. nz/store/2006/07/ national-population-projections04%28base%29-51 -mr.htm.

———. (2006). Demographic aspects of New Zealand's ageing population (March).

———. (2007). New Zealand income survey (June).

Toder, Eric & Strachey Khitatrakun. (2006). *Final report to inland revenue: KiwiSaver evaluation literature review*. Tax Policy Center (December 4).

[SSA] U.S. Social Security Administration. (2007). *Social Security Programs throughout the World: Asia and the Pacific, 2006* (March).

End Notes

[1] In New Zealand, the term "superannuation" means retirement.

[2] This figure has been raised to 66 percent during the term of the current government as a result of an agreement with a coalition party. The floor is set by law at 65 percent (MSD 2007); according to the New Zealand Superannuation Act 2001, average wage is determined by the last Quarterly Employment Survey published by the Department of Statistics before March 1 each year. For more information on the average wage, see Statistics (2007).

[3] For more information on the government's contribution to the NZSF, see sections 42 and 43 of the New Zealand Superannuation Act 2001.

[4] A portion of NZS funding will continue to come from general revenues.

[5] For an evaluation of the NZSF, see Littlewood (2005) and St. John (2001).

[6] See Le and others (2007).

[7] The 2003 report was produced by the Periodic Report Group, a panel of public- and private-sector experts that reviewed New Zealand's retirement income policy every 6 years. The review function was transferred to the Retirement Commissioner who presented her first report at the end of 2007. After that, the Commissioner is required to present a report every 3 years (Retirement Commission 2007a).

[8] As of 2005, about 50 percent of the U.S. labor force participated in some type of employer-sponsored retirement plan (Costo 2006).

[9] Unless otherwise noted, the source for the information on KiwiSaver in this section is http://www.kiwisaver.govt. nz.

[10] This includes new entrants to the labor force and workers who are starting a new job.

[11] For example, if the employer contributes 4 percent of the employee's earnings, the entire 4 percent is tax-exempt to the employer. If the employer and the employee each contribute 2 percent of the employee's earnings, the employer's 2 percent contribution was tax-exempt. Employers pay a special tax called specified superannuation contribution withholding tax (SSCWT) on the rest of their contributions to an employee's account.

[12] This measure was added in December 2007.

[13] According to the law, the definition of serious illness is either permanently or totally disabled or near death.

[14] Providers include banks, insurers, and management companies.

[15] The Ministry of Economic Development has selected six default providers (New Zealand Government 2007).

[16] Other functions of the Retirement Commission include collecting research on retirement planning behaviour and attitudes and providing information that aids development of national policies impacting on retirement. For more information go to http://www.retirement.org.nz/retirement_commission_home.html.

[17] In New Zealand, investment earnings are taxed.

[18] Close to 20 percent of these workers are younger than age 25 and more than half are younger than age 45.

In: International Social Security: Agreements... ISBN: 978-1-61761-430-9
Editors: Nicole E. Pampino

Chapter 6

THE EVOLUTION OF JAPANESE EMPLOYER-SPONSORED RETIREMENT PLANS

David Rajnes

SUMMARY

This article examines the development of Japanese voluntary employer-sponsored retirement plans with an emphasis on recent trends. Until 2001, companies in Japan offered retirement benefits as lump-sum severance payments and/or benefits from one of two types of defined benefit (DB) pension plans. One type of DB plan was based on the occupational pension model used in the United States before the adoption of the Employee Retirement Income Security Act of 1974 (ERISA), but lacked the funding, vesting, and other protective features contained in ERISA. The other type of DB plan allowed companies to opt out of the earnings-related portion of social security, commonly referred to as "contracting out."

Landmark laws passed in 2001 introduced a new generation of occupational retirement plans to employers and employees. One law increased funding requirements and enhanced employee protections for employer-sponsored DB plans, while a second law introduced defined contribution (DC) plans for several reasons, chiefly to increase retirement savings and help boost Japanese financial markets. These laws complemented earlier changes in the tax code and financial accounting standards already affecting employer-sponsored retirement plans. As a result, new retirement plan designs will replace most prereform era company retirement plans by 2012.

In 2001, the experience of 401(k) plans in the United States, where 42 million participants had accumulated more than $1.8 trillion in assets over 20 years, attracted considerable attention among Japanese lawmakers finalizing provisions of the DC pension law. Even with government support and encouragement from the financial services industry, Japanese companies have not adopted these new DC plans in large numbers. As a result, occupational retirement plans in Japan have remained predominantly DB—a surprising development in light of the shift in a number of countries from DB to DC plans observed in recent decades. However, recent proposals to make DC plans more attractive to employers in Japan are likely to be implemented in the near future.

This article

- summarizes the Japanese retirement system, with an emphasis on private-sector employees, and the complementary role played by voluntary employer-sponsored retirement plans;
- describes the financial pressures that faced retirement plan sponsors in the late twentieth century and the factors motivating the reform of Japanese voluntary retirement plans;
- examines the 2001 legislative changes that have transformed company retirement plans; and
- concludes with a review of trends and recent developments in employer-sponsored retirement plans since the implementation of the 2001 pension laws.

Japan's Retirement System

A combination of low birthrates (1.26 children per woman of child-bearing age in 2005, well below the 2.1 needed to maintain population size) and gains in life expectancy at birth (rising from 76.9 years in 1980 to the current 82.6 years) has made Japan one of the world's oldest societies. According to government estimates, the percentage of Japanese aged 65 or older will climb from the current 20 percent of the population to nearly 36 percent by 2050, while the working-aged population, aged 15 to 64, will decrease from roughly 66 percent to about half the population (Dow Jones

International News 2006). If these trends continue, the population will decline from its peak of 128 million in 2005 to 101 million persons by 2050. To counteract effects on social security finances from these projected demographic developments, the country initiated a series of major reforms in 1994, 1999, and 2004 to limit social security retirement program expenditures.

Japan's retirement system is largely comprised of a social security system and employer-sponsored retirement plans. Under the social security system, private- sector employees and the self-employed are treated differently (U.S. Social Security Administration 2007; Yamamoto and Fukawa 2003; Kabe 2006).

The National Pension (NP), a partially funded compulsory system, covers the self-employed, farmers, and others, aged 20-60, who are not full-time employees. These individuals contribute a flat-rate monthly contribution, which was 13,860 yen (US$128) in April 2006. The NP system provides a pension benefit proportional to the number of years of contribution. The full monthly NP benefit, available after 40 years of contributions, amounts to about 66,000 yen (US$61 1). The eligible age for full NP benefits, currently age 62, has been increasing by 1 year every 3 years since 2001, targeted to reach age 65 by 2013. All NP administrative costs and one-third of NP benefits are subsidized by tax revenues.[1]

For full-time private-sector employees in Japan, there is a two-tiered social security system, known as the Employees' Pension Insurance (EPI). The EPI includes a flat-rate first tier, with contribution and benefit features identical to the NP program, and an earnings-related second tier. The overall EPI contribution rate (combined employer and employee) is 14.29 percent of employee pretax earnings. Since October 2004, this contribution rate of 13.58 has been rising in increments of 0.35 percent each year and will reach 18.30 percent in 2017. Contributions are levied and benefits are calculated based on monthly earnings ranging from a minimum of 98,000 yen (US$822) to a maximum of 620,000 yen (US$5,197). The earnings- related benefit equals 0.55 percent of the employee's average monthly wage indexed over his or her working career multiplied by the number of covered years (Sakamoto 2005).

Under the EPI system, the average replacement rate for male employees with a contribution record of 40 years (taking into account the flat-rate first tier and the earnings-related second tier and assuming average earnings during that time) is approximately 43 percent. The average EPI household replacement rate for a male employee with the same earnings profile, but with a nonworking spouse, is approximately 59 percent. These replacement rates are projected to decline gradually to 36 percent by 2023 for male employees and to about 50 percent by 2023 for households (Sakamoto 2005).[2]

The current eligible age for full EPI benefits will rise from age 60 to age 65 in the coming decades. For men, the earliest age to receive retirement benefits will increase by 1 year every 3 years from 2013 until it reaches age 65 in 2025; for women, the earliest age to receive benefits will rise by 1 year every 3 years starting in 2018 until it reaches age 65 in 2030 (Kabe 2006).

Voluntary employer-sponsored retirement plans in Japan complement the country's two-tiered social security system. Historically, companies have generally rewarded departing employees for their long service to the firm with lump-sum severance payments. After that employee benefit lost its tax advantages in 2002, the popularity of employer-paid lump-sum severance payments declined. Since the 1 960s, employers began to offer defined benefit (DB) pension plans in addition to or as a substitute for, their lump-sum severance programs. In 2005, about 14 million of 37 million salaried employees were covered by employer- sponsored DB plans. These pension plan assets accounted for 60 trillion yen (US$517 billion) out of a total 266 trillion yen (US$2 trillion) for all private and public pension funds that same year (Y. Watanabe 2006-2007).

Employer-Sponsored Plans before the 2001 Reform

Before 2001, Japanese employers generally used three types of voluntary retirement arrangements for departing employees: an unfunded book-reserve plan providing lump-sum payments and two DB plans, a Tax-Qualified Pension Plan and an Employee Pension Fund. Both DB plan designs received preferential tax treatment and required that third party administrators manage the plan assets. Table 1 indicates the major characteristics of these retirement plans.

Book-Reserve Plans (BRP)

Changes to the tax code in 1952 provided incentives for firms to establish an internal account or BRP for their severance pay program, enabling firms to make periodic tax-favored contributions to their BRP plan.[3] However, since firms were under no legal obligation to set aside funds to offset the firm's accumulating liabilities to employees, nearly all BRPs have been unfunded (N. Watanabe 1998).

Tax-Qualified Pension Plans (TQPPs)

TQPPs were introduced in 1962 and were based on the DB pension model then used in the United States. A company with 15 or more employees could establish a TQPP with the approval of the National Tax Administration, an agency of the Ministry of Finance. Employer contributions, either a specified amount or percentage of payroll, are deductible as a business expense. TQPP benefits are based on years of service, using a flat benefit or an earnings-related formula and may be offered as either a monthly annuity or a lump sum. Eligible employees select lump-sum payments over annuities more than 80 percent of the time (Katsumata 2005). In addition, TQPP plans must be managed by an outside financial contractor—either a trust bank or a life insurance company.

EMPLOYEES' PENSION FUND (EPF)

A second DB plan design, and one closely linked to the earnings-related portion of the EPI system, is the EPF plan. Since October 1966, companies could partially "contract out" of social security by setting up an independent EPF corporation to manage the earnings-related (EPI) portion of social security. The phrase "contract out" means that a firm—provided that its union members (if any) agree and both the Ministry of Health and Welfare and the Ministry of Finance approve—may pay a reduced social security contribution in exchange for providing a pension benefit that replaces the earnings-related EPI social security benefit. The EPF plan must also provide an overall pension benefit higher than the earnings-related portion of EPI (Hewitt Associates 2003). This additional EPF benefit originally equaled 30 percent, but the government reduced the additional EPF benefit from 30 percent to 10 percent in 2001 to discourage companies from terminating their EPF plans.[4]

Table 1. Major Japanese Employer-Sponsored Retirement Plans in 2001, by Year Started and Plan Characteristics

Type of plan or fund	Year started	Plan characteristics
Book Reserve Plan (BRP)	1952	Traditional way of providing severance payment to departing worker
		Benefit in the form of a lump sum
		Unfunded pay-as-you-go method financed by employers alone
		Earmarked reserves as a liability on company balance sheet
		Loss of tax-deductible status beginning in 2002
Tax-Qualified Pension Plan (TQPP)	1962	Based on U.S. Defined Benefit model
		Plan must be externally funded and assets managed by contract with life insurance companies and trust banks
		Employer's contributions are 100 percent tax deductible as a business expense
		Plan must contain a provision for annuities, although a lump-sum option is provided
		No tax on investment earnings
		Used primarily by small and medium-sized firms with more than 15 employees
		Regulated by the Ministry of Finance
Employees' Pension Fund (EPF)	1966	Defined Benefit plan contracted out from social security
		Must be established as a legal entity independent from the employer
		In return for a lower social security contribution, firms must provide benefits equivalent to the earnings-related portion of social security and a supplementary benefit (lump sum or annuity) financed by the employer
		Plan must be funded and assets held outside the firm in a trust fund or in an insurance contract
		Life annuities must be provided
		Tax treatment virtually the same as TQPP
		Used by large companies and by multiemployer groups
		Regulated by the Ministry of Health, Labor and Welfare

Source: Compiled by author.

Table 2. Japanese Employer-Sponsored Retirement Plans, 1997 and 2003 (in Percents)

Number of employees in firm	Percent of firms with—				Type of retirement plan offered					
	Retirement plans		No plans		BRP lump sum only		Annuity (EPF or TQPP)		Both (BRP/ Annuity	
	1997	2003	1997	2003	1997	2003	1997	2003	1997	2003
Total	100.0	100.0	100.0	100.0	100.0	100.0	100.0	100.0	100.0	100.0
30–99	85.7	84.7	14.3	15.3	48.1	45.8	15.6	15.5	22.1	23.5
100–299	95.9	89.5	4.1	10.5	33.8	31.1	22.9	19.3	40.0	39.1
300–999	97.7	95.7	2.3	4.3	17.2	21.7	30.5	25.3	50.1	48.7
1,000 or more	99.5	97.1	0.5	2.9	9.5	10.7	22.5	18.5	67.4	67.9

Source: Japanese Ministry of Health, Labor, and Welfare (2003, 2004).

Note: BRP = Book Reserve Plan; EPF = Employee Pension Fund; TQPP = Tax Qualified Pension Fund.

The EPF plan must achieve at least the government- specified annual nominal yield. Initially, the government set a guaranteed rate of 5.5 percent, but allowed this rate to decline in the 1 990s to match the fall in Japan's interest rates. The government reduced the guaranteed nominal rate for EPF plans to 4.5 percent in 1994 and then to 1.5 percent in 1999 as the economy weakened (Dai-Ichi 2006). Should an EPF plan become over-funded, plan sponsors could either reduce their employer contribution or improve plan benefits (Clark 1991).

Because of concerns about the financial stability of EPF plans, the Japanese government required a minimum number of participants in an EPF plan based on whether the plan sponsor was a single company or a group of companies. The volatility of plan finances is larger for plans composed of small companies since these small companies have a greater risk of bankruptcy than do large companies. For that reason, EPF plans composed of small companies must have a higher minimum number of employees than that required of EPF plans where only larger companies participate (Turner and Rajnes 1995). In 2005, the government raised the minimum number from 500 to 1,000 employees for a single-employer sponsor from 800 to 1,000 employees for jointly affiliated sponsor companies and from 3,000 to 5,000 employees for a group sponsor of smaller companies (categorized by industry, occupation, or region). Given this size requirement, the number of employees in EPF plans tends to be larger than in TQPP plans (Japan Ministry of Health, Labor, and Welfare 2005b).

Due to the contracted-out nature of these liabilities, the government treats EPF plans as quasi-public entities with very detailed administration and management rules (Usuki 2003). For example, EPF rules require plan sponsors to distribute at least half of the retirement benefit as an annuity unless a pensioner requests a lump sum. Originally, EPF investments were restricted to a list of approved investments managed by trust banks and insurance companies, but those restrictions were abolished in 1997 (Watanabe, Y. 2006-2007).

EPFs also are required to participate in the national association of EPF plans, known as the Pension Fund Association (PFA). The PFA serves two major purposes. First, it insures against loss of benefits in the event of a plan sponsor's bankruptcy.[5] Second, it assures there is no loss of benefits for employees who switch employers, since the accumulated contributions of departing employees are transferred to the PFA to manage, thus providing a portable pension system for those changing jobs (Turner and Rajnes 1995; N. Watanabe 1996).

By 2000, employee coverage for firms with at least 30 employees using one of these three types of occupational retirement plans was close to 90 percent, although coverage by a TQPP or EPF plan offering an annuity was only around 50 percent. Table 2 shows the percentage of firms with 30 or more employees offering a retirement plan in 1997 and 2003. These data indicate that larger firms were more likely to offer a retirement plan than were smaller firms. Comparable data are not available for firms with fewer than 30 employees.

Table 2 also shows the type of retirement plan offered—BRPs, EPFs, or TQPPs—and percentage change by firm size from 1997 to 2003. Retirement benefits offered by smaller firms were more likely to consist only of a BRP plan. Overall, the percentage of firms offering a retirement plan decreased slightly from 1997 to 2003, as did the percentage of firms offering an annuity-based (EPF or TQPP) retirement plan. No consistent pattern by firm size was evident regarding either the BRP or the combination (BRP/ annuity) retirement plans. While the use of BRP plans declined overall, the percentage of firms with more than 300 employees offering these plans actually increased slightly. Nearly half of the firms with less than 100 employees offered a BRP as the only retirement plan, and this percentage decreased as the firm size grew. While the percentage of firms with both an annuity-based (EPF or TQPP) plan and a BRP retirement plan increased somewhat, this change occurred only among the largest (1,000 or more employees) and the smallest (from 30 to 99 employees) firms studied.

COMPANY RETIREMENT PLANS ENCOUNTER PROBLEMS IN THE 1990S

Following a period of high investment and employment growth beginning in the late 1980s, the Japanese business sector entered a prolonged slump in 1992 that lasted for more than a decade. Lower profitability prevented many plan sponsors from increasing contributions to their retirement plans to offset the shortfall in plan investment earnings needed to maintain retirement plan benefits. As economic stagnation persisted throughout the 1990s, many companies took cost-cutting steps, including employee layoffs, the increased use of part-time employees, and the reduction or elimination of retirement plans.

Defined benefit plans (EPF and TQPP) and membership peaked between 1994 and 1997 before declining thereafter. For example, the number of TQPP participants declined from a high of 10.8 million in 1995 to 9.2 million in 2001. The number of TQPP plans (referred to as "contracts") exhibited a similar pattern, increasing to 92,467 plans in 1993 before declining to 73,582 plans in 2001. The number of EPF plan participants declined from its highest level of 12.2 million in 1997 to 10.9 million in 2001. The number of EPF plans increased to 1,883 in 1996 before declining to 1,737 in 2001 (Table 3).

In contrastto the general decline in the number of DB plans and DB plan members, total assets under management for both TQPP and EPF plans grew throughout the period from 1991 to 2001. Total assets managed by EPF plans expanded steadily throughout the 1990s and reached 58.3 trillion yen (US$482.1 billion) in 2001, while TQPP plan assets rose to 22.7 trillion yen in 2001. Much of the explanation for the continued rise in asset values stems from the fact that plan sponsors recorded higher book values on their financial statements instead of the lower market values, as reflected by declining financial markets at that time.[6] Therefore, one must exercise caution in interpreting the steady rise in managed plan assets for both EPF and TQPP plans throughout the 1990s.

Before 1990, EPF plans earned roughly 8.0 percent to 10.0 percent in nominal terms each year on their assets, well above the 5.5 nominal target rate of return required by the government, while inflation-adjusted rates of return remained well below those yields much of the time. After inflation dipped below 3.0 percent after 1981, the spread between nominal and real yields narrowed significantly. Both nominal and real yields fell dramatically with the decline in Japan's economy around 1989 and remained below 5.0 percent in the 1990s except for 1995 and 1999. Chart 1 shows the variability in nominal and real asset returns from 1975 to 2005 for existing EPF plans and from 1990 to 2005 for former EPF plans managed by the Pension Fund Association.

By the late 1990s, with declining asset values and a rise in employer contribution holidays, the estimated underfunding of employer-sponsored (EPF and TQPP) pension plans reached roughly between 40 trillion yen (US$404 billion) and 60 trillion yen (US$485 billion) (Clark and Mitchell 2002). At the same time, the unfunded liabilities of BRP plans represented another US$324 billion to US$404 billion (Goldman Sachs 1999). The funding levels of retirement plans worsened when both nominal and real investment yields turned negative during 2000-2002. By 2001, 96 percent of corporate pension funds were underfunded (Nakamoto 2003).

In 2000, Japan adopted new accounting rules that exposed the extent of pension underfunding in many company plans (Usuki 2003; Nakada 2004). Under the old accounting rules, corporate pension plan shortfalls did not appear on corporate financial statements as a liability. The new rules, however, require companies with 300 or more employees to disclose unfunded pension and retirement obligations on their balance sheets (Takahashi 2006). At the same time, the government allowed the discount rate pension plans used for calculating pension liabilities to float according to the nominal yield of less risky long-term investment vehicles, such as government bonds, effectively increasing the amount required to make employer-sponsored pension funds solvent (Shimada 2002).

2001 Reform of Employer-Sponsored Retirement Plans

Recognizing the growing financial pressures on retirement plan sponsors and their problems funding those plans, the Japanese legislature passed two pieces of legislation in 2001 that significantly affected what retirement benefits employers could offer employees. One law changed the rules governing DB plans, included an option for EPF funds to return their assets related to social security contributions to the government, introduced hybrid plans and other new DB plan designs, and scheduled a date for the elimination of TQPP plans. A second law introduced defined contribution (DC) plans as a new pension plan option for employers.

Defined Benefit Corporate Pension Law (2001)

The objectives of the Defined Benefit Corporate Pension Law of 2001 were to unify the regulations and tax provisions of DB plans while enhancing the retirement income security of DB plan participants (Urata 2001). Specifically, the law provided for a greater variety of DB fund designs than was available with the existing EPF system and imposed stricter funding rules for employee benefits than those under TQPP plans. In addition, the DB law defined fiduciary duties of pension plan sponsors for the first time, including greater disclosure requirements of plan operations to plan participants. The law also introduced rules for transferring rights and obligations from one type of pension fund to another, including the conversion of a DB plan to a DC plan. Table 4 summarizes the key provisions of the law outlined in the text below.

The DB law permitted some EPF plan sponsors to transfer their EPF obligations for contracted out benefits back to the government. In addition, the law created a fund-type DB plan with a design similar to an EPF plan but lacking the contracting out option. Also, the law specified that no TQPP plans could be created after April 2002; existing TQPP plans must eventually, and transfer their assets to another fund type or distribute them to employee participants within 10 years. For that reason, the DB law created a contract-type DB plan, which resembles the TQPP type, but has stricter rules on reporting, disclosure, vesting, and funding.

Finally, the 2001 DB law permitted companies to create the cash balance plan, a hybrid pension which combines features of a DB and a DC plan design. Under the cash balance design, each employee has a notional account into which the employer credits a fixed percentage of the basic salary and an annual interest payment. The periodic interest credited to the employee account must be one of the following:

> (a) fixed rate; (b) national bond rate or another common index such as the consumer price index (CPI); (c) an interest rate combining (a) and (b); or (d) a floating rate using a national bond rate as a floor and a combined fixed/ notional rate as a ceiling (Endo 2002, Fujiwara 2006).

Table 3. Japanese Employer-Sponsored Pension Plans, by Number of Participants, and Assets Prior to Pension Reform, 1991–2001

Year	Employees pension funds			Tax-qualified pension plans		
	Number of funds	Number of participants (in thousands)	Assets under management (in billion yen)	Number of contracts	Number of participants (in thousands)	Assets under management (in billion yen)
1991	1,593	10,678	28,800	90,434	9,770	14,100
1992	1,735	11,571	32,184	92,082	10,400	15,029
1993	1,804	11,919	35,416	92,467	10,600	16,071
1994	1,842	12,051	38,426	92,355	10,751	16,957
1995	1,878	12,130	41,775	91,465	10,776	17,801
1996	1,883	12,096	44,959	90,239	10,626	18,466
1997	1,874	12,254	48,695	88,312	10,432	19,156
1998	1,858	12,002	51,281	85,047	10,297	19,988
1999	1,832	11,692	55,486	81,605	10,011	21,137
2000	1,801	11,396	58,017	77,555	9,656	22,358
2001	1,737	10,871	58,297	73,582	9,167	22,719

Source: Usuki (2003) for Assets under management, 1992-2001; remaining data taken from the Japanese Ministry of Health, Labor and Welfare (2005a).

Note: Data are as of the end of the fiscal year. Japanese fiscal years run from April 1 to March 31.

Additional changes in the 2001 DB law affected funding, benefits, and plan termination. First, funding levels for new DB plans must satisfy EPF plan requirements, including the requirement that plans issue a statement of vested benefits and a present-value calculation of vested benefits. If a pension plan is underfunded, plan sponsors must develop a schedule to restore plan assets to the minimum funding level through increased contributions and/or accelerating the amortization of unfunded liabilities. Plan sponsors may use a funding surplus to take a contribution holiday.

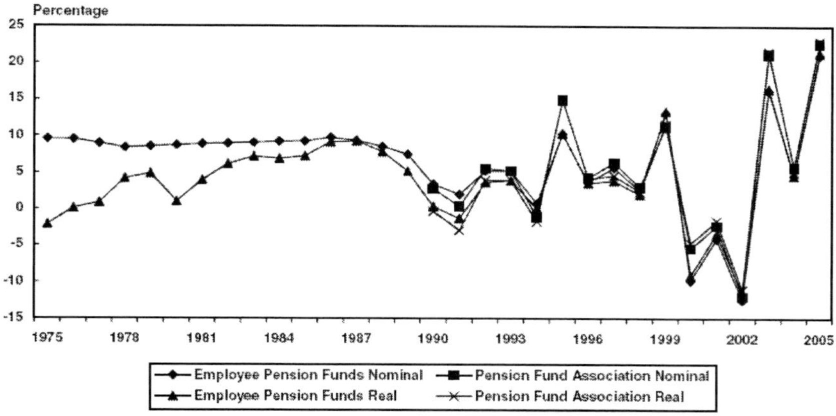

Source: Pension Fund Association, *The Basic Statistics about Company Pension Plans, various years. Pension Fund Association, Annual Report of Employees' Pension Funds*, various years.

Note: Annual data reflect yields for fiscal years specified. The Japanese fiscal year runs from April 1 to March 31.

Chart 1. Investment performance for Japanese corporate pension plans, 1975–2005 (nominal and real yields)

Table 4. Defined Benefit Corporate Pension Law 2001, by Key Provisions and Affected Areas

Affected areas	Key Provisions
Choice of Plans	Three new Defined Benefit (DB) plan types created with differing features:
	(1) Contract-type DB plan
	Similar to Tax Qualified Pension Plan (TQPP) but more tightly regulated (funding standards, fiduciary duties, and disclosure)
	No minimum number of employees required
	Plan sponsor establishes a plan by contracting with trustee companies
	Employer contributions paid to trustee
	Pension assets transferrable to another plan
	Trustee responsible for management of pension assets and payment of pension benefits
	No contracting out feature
	(2) Fund-type DB plan

Table 4. (Continued)

Affected areas	Key Provisions
	Similar to Employee Pension Fund (EPF) plan but no option to "contract out" of social security system
	Minimum number of employees required to establish a plan is 300
	Employer or a group of employers can establish a plan to manage contributed assets or contract with trustee companies
	Plan is a separate legal entity independent of firm
	Employer contributions paid to trustee who pays benefits
	Trustee responsible for management of pension assets and payment of pension benefits
	Plan is administered by a board of directors and an assembly of delegates
	(3) Cash balance plan
	Each participant has a hypothetical account balance
	The two amounts credited to the account each year are contributions based on the participant's wage or salary and guaranteed interest with the rate specified by the plan
	Plan sponsor bears investment risk and must pay additional contributions if managed assets do not outperform guaranteed rate
Contributions	Employer-only contributions (tax-deductible) unless plan regulations specify otherwise Additional contributions required to make up for any plan underfunding
Plan establishment	Plan sponsor needs assent of at least half of employees or union approval to establish the plan Approval needed from the Ministry of Health, Labor and Welfare (MHLW) to establish the plan according
	Converting plan assets to another type of corporate DB plan permissible
Plan conversions	TQPPs must be converted by March 31, 2012 to ensure employer contributions remain tax-ded ductible Conversion options include EPF plan, mutual aid plan, or one of the three new plan types (see above)
Employee Pension Fund	EPF plans contracting out of social security given opportunity to transfer assets for that liability back to the government
	4-step process established with rules for steps 1 and 2 included in the 2001 law and rules for steps 3 and 4 implemented in 2003:
	Step 1–employer gets approval from employees and then applies to MHLW for exemption from future contracting-out obligations
	Step 2–establish payment of social security contributions by employer and employees at the full (non-contracted-out) rates

Table 4. (Continued)

Affected areas	Key Provisions
	Step 3–data reconciliation for past EPF service with the government and the Pension Fund Association
	Step 4–final government approval for the separation of assets and their transfer back to the government

Sources: Freshfields (2003), Mizuho Financial Group (2001), Morito (2001), and Hewitt Associates (2003).

Second, regulations specify that a minimum benefit and the benefit formula must be considered "reasonable" after taking into account an employee's years of service, salary, and so forth. A plan must pay old-age benefits as an annuity, although a portion may be paid as a lump sum. Survivor and disability benefits are not required but may be available to participants at the plan sponsor's discretion. The law defined a cash balance benefit formula for plans converted from a traditional DB plan to a cash balance plan.

Finally, a plan sponsor may terminate a plan only with the consent of the relevant labor union or employee representatives and approval by the Ministry of Health, Labor and Welfare (Japan MHLW). At termination, the plan sponsor is required to make up any funding shortfall.

DEFINED CONTRIBUTION PLAN LAW (2001)

The Japanese government supported passage of the Defined Contribution Plan Law in 2001 for several reasons (Katsumata 2005; Fujiwara 2003; McLellan 2004). First, unlike DB plans, the DC law gave employers more retirement plan choices, including limiting their pension obligations under the new DC plans. Second, Japan's increasingly mobile labor force appeared compatible with the portability of individual accounts. Third, DC plans, it was thought, would encourage individuals to focus on retirement planning in anticipation of the scheduled reduction of social security benefits previously approved in 2000.

Finally, the Japanese government hoped the introduction of DC plans might stimulate the flow of individual retirement account assets into Japanese financial markets. To many observers in Japan at that time, the expanding U.S. economy and stock market boom of the 1 990s appeared driven, in part, by the growth of DC plans, primarily 40 1(k) plans, so the introduction of a 401(k)-

style pension plan surfaced as a potential remedy to boost the weak Japanese stock market by raising the demand for Japanese stocks.

Provisions under the new DC law established two types of DC plans: a corporate DC plan and an individual DC plan. Details on both plan types are contained in Table 5.

Employers establishing a corporate DC plan, after obtaining employee approval, usually contract out responsibility for administering the plan to a third- party administrator (such as a qualified bank or insurance firm). These employers contribute a fixed monthly tax-deductible contribution on behalf of their employees. Initially, the maximum allowable (nontaxable) annual contribution for each employee was set at 216,000 yen (US$1,880) if the company established a DC plan in addition to an existing DB plan. If the company had no DB plan it was set at 432,000 yen (U.S.$3,759). As part of the 2004 social security reform, these contribution limits increased to 276,000 yen (US$2,344) per year for employees with access to a qualified DB plan and to 552,000 yen (US$4,690) per year for employees without access to a qualified DB plan. Employees may not contribute to a corporate DC plan.

An individual DC plan is available to self-employed workers and employees who do not have access to a company pension plan. These individuals may apply to join the National Pension Fund Association, which contracts on behalf of its members with trustee companies to manage their members' DC assets. Self-employed workers pay a tax deductible monthly contribution up to an annual limit of 816,000 yen (US$6,866), while employees without access to a company retirement plan may contribute up to an annual limit of 180,000 yen (US$1,515). The contribution limit of employees in companies without a retirement plan was raised in October 2004 to 216,000 yen per year (US$1,773).

Below are provisions introduced by the 2001 DC law.

Eligibility. To be eligible for coverage by a DC plan, workers aged 60 or younger must participate in the social security system. Government workers and spouses of company employees are ineligible.

Vesting. After 3 years of service with an employer, an employee's corporate DC plan account is non-forfeitable.

Investments. Participants may select from among three or more investment alternatives that must contain at least one capital guaranteed product. A registered company (third party administrator) provides the range of investment products, information to improve financial literacy, and administration of participant investments.

Benefit Distribution. Funds can be withdrawn beginning at age 60 with 10 years of contributions, but must begin no later than age 70. Benefits may be claimed either as an annuity or as a lump sum. For those contributing less than 10 years, the withdrawal date may be delayed, but must occur no later than age 66.

Portability. Employees must transfer their accumulated assets to their new employer's DC plan after changing jobs or to an individual DC plan if the new employer does not offer a corporate DC plan, unless the worker is older than age 60.

Table 5. Defined Contribution Corporate Pension Law, effective October 1, 2001

Affected areas	Key Provisions
Plan establishment	Two new Defined Contribution (DC) plan types created:
	(1) Corporate DC plan
	Empoyees eligible if employer sponsors plan
	Requires assent of majority of employees or union representative as to plan rules
	No minimum number of employees required
	Employer appoints trustees (usually trust banks or insurance companies) to administer pension assets
	Plan sponsor responsible for providing financial education information to participants
	Employer only pays a fixed percentage of salary or a fixed monthly contribution (tax-deductible) on behalf of employees
	Maximum allowable contribution for each employee varies (¥216,000 (US$1,843) for companies also having a Defined Benefit (DB) plan and ¥432,000 (US$3,684) for companies without a DB plan)
	Vesting rules vary across plans but plans must have 100 percent vesting after 3 years and may have partial vesting within that time
	Companies are permitted to convert from a severance pay (book reserve) plan to a DC plan with benefits calculated on the basis of new contributions and/or past service credits from old plan, plus interest
	(2) Individual DC plan

Table 5. (Continued)

Affected areas	Key Provisions
	Available to self-employed workers and others not participating in a corporate pension plan, but must be covered by social socurity
	Individual can apply to join the National Pension Fund Association (NFPA) which acts as trustee on behalf of members
	Employees have their employer deduct contributions from pay and send them to the NFPA
	Self-employed persons remit contributions directly to NFPA
	Individual selects plan administrator who prepares a packaged product containing certain investment options
	Individual decides how much to contribute and pays it on a monthly basis up to certain annual limits (up to ¥816,000 (US$6,959) for self-employed workers and up to ¥180,000 (US$1,535) for employees ineligible to receive pension benefits)
Benefits	Three types of benefits (old age, disability, and survivors) payable in a lump sum; benefits may vary depending on plan rules
Taxation	Contributions are fully tax-deductible and investment earnings are tax-deferred
Investments	Individual participant selects from among at least three investment options products (one of which guarantees principal)
	Participant can rebalance portfolio as often as once every 3 months Third parties administering employee investments and providing investment information must register with the Ministry of Health, Labor and Welfare
Age	Eligible persons include those younger than age 60 and covered by the social security system Persons aged 60 or older eligible for old-age benefit with 10 years of participation Persons may start receiving benefits as early as age 60, but must begin receiving them at age 70
Rollover accounts	Mandatory rollover of plan assets (individual accounts) for those aged 60 or younger upon termination of employment or change of employer to new employer's DC plan or to individual DC plan account
	The exception to mandatory rollover is loss of eligibility within 3 years of becoming a participant

Sources: Freshfields (2003), Mizuho Financial Group (2001), Takayama (2005), Urata (2001), and Morito (2001).

POSTREFORM DEVELOPMENTS IN EMPLOYER-SPONSERED PLANS

In the 6 years since Japan implemented its 2001 DB and DC pension laws, the mix of employer-sponsored retirement plans offered in Japan has changed significantly, and overall employee coverage has declined. This outcome can be attributed to post-2001 changes in the tax code and other laws affecting employer- sponsored pensions. Pension experts expect further pension changes based on a government review released in July 2007.

Trends in the Postreform ERA

Since 2001, the number of plans and participants in prereform retirement plans, such as EPF and TQPP plans, have declined as new plan types (DB and DC) were adopted (Table 6).[7] By 2005, the downward trend in DB plans reversed, while the total number of DB and DC plans being offered by employers increased slightly. Table 6 presents similar patterns of decline and growth in the number of retirement plan participants beginning in 2004. On balance, employer- sponsored retirement plans have remained largely DB in design.

From 2001 to 2006, the number of EPF plans fell 61 percent (from 1,737 to 672), while the number of plan participants declined more than 50 percent (10.9 million to 5.3 million). Government statistics show that nearly 80 percent of former EPF plans converted to a new type of DB plan allowed under the 2001 law, a small portion of EPF plan assets were transferred to a DC plan, and less than 20 percent of EPF plans were dissolved (Shimizu 2005).

Most of the decrease in EPF plans and plan assets occurred after 2003 when many EPF plan sponsors began to transfer their obligations for the contracted- out EPI (earnings-related) social security portion of the EPF fund back to the government to remove significant pension liabilities from corporate pension balance sheets and thus improve firm credit ratings (Sato 2005). This process involves several steps. First, the Ministry of Health, Labor, and Welfare must approve an employer's request to return the contracted out portion of social security. Once approved, plan sponsors then transfer the accumulated social security-related funds back to the government.

After the transfer, a plan sponsor can convert its remaining DB plan assets to one of the two new DB plans or the new DC corporate plan.

Table 6. Post-Reform Trends in Japanese Employer-Sponsored Pension Plans, 2001 –2006

Year	Total	Types of DB plans				
		EPF	TQPP	DB contract and fund type plans	DB fund type plan	Total DC corporate
	Number of pension plans					
2001	75,319	1,737	73,582	. . .	. . .	70
2002	68,412	1,656	66,741	15	0	361
2003	60,835	1,357	59,162	165	151	845
2004	54,591	838	52,761	479	513	1,402
2005	47,207	687	45,090	833	597	1,866
2006	47,432	672[a]	45,090[b]	1,067[a]	603[a]	2,191[c]
	Number of participants (in thousands)					
2001	20,038	10,871	9,167	. . .	. . .	88
2002	18,972	10,386	8,586	. . .	. . .	325
2003	16,151	8,351	7,770	30	. . .	708
2004	14,032	6,152	6,530	1,350	. . .	1,255
2005	14,827	5,300	5,687	3,840	. . .	1,733
2006	14,810	5,300[a]	5,670[b]	3,840[b]	. . .	2,106[d]

Source: Ministry of Health, Labour and Welfare (2005a) for all EPF and TQPP through 2004 and for other data through 2003; remaining data obtained from sources noted.

Notes: Defined Benefit Plans started from April 1, 2002; Defined Contribution Corporate Plans started from October 1, 2001

Data through 2005 reflect figures at end of fiscal year. Japanese fiscal years run from April 1 to March 31.

DB = Defined Benefit plan; EPF = Employee Pension Fund; TQPP = Tax-Qualified Pension plan; DC = Defined Contribution plan; . . . = not applicable.

a. Data as of September 1, 2006 (Pension Fund Association).

b. Data as of July 31, 2006 (Pension Fund Association).

c. Data as of January 31, 2007 (Ministry of Health, Labor and Welfare).

d. Data as of December 31, 2006 (Ministry of Health, Labor and Welfare).

The government's buy-back program was quite generous and nearly all employers with single-employer EPF plans took advantage of this program. For EPFs with multiple plan sponsors, negotiating an agreement to return the contracted-out assets to the government has been difficult because the process often requires protracted coordination and cooperation among participating companies. Thus, these employers cannot withdraw easily from their EPF arrangement since they must receive approval from three-quarters of participating employers as well as their own employees (McGuinness 2003; McLellan 2005; Fujiwara 2006).

The 2001 DB law requires plan sponsors to convert TQPP plans into another type of pension plan by 2012. As evident in the data in Table 6, the decline of TQPP plans has been almost as dramatic as that for EPF plans. However, the relatively smaller firm size associated with most TQPP plans may explain why over 60 percent of these plans still have not converted. Close to 45,100 TQPP plans with around 5.7 million participants were operational in 2006 compared with nearly 73,600 such plans covering almost 9.2 million workers in 2001. Some TQPP plan sponsors have transferred their TQPP contracts to the government-run Mutual Aid Organization for Employees' Retirement Allowances for businesses with less than 300 million yen (US$2.6 million) or fewer than 300 employees (Freshfields 2003). By November 2005, the number of TQPP contract transfers to the government reached 7,447 plans (Arimori 2006). Some employers converted their TQPP plans, which resulted in 627 additional DC plans by early 2005 and 358 contract-type DB plans by the end of 2004 (Shimizu 2005). Plan sponsors terminated the remaining TQPP plans.

Like TQPP plans, book-reserve plans (BRPs) lost their tax-favored status as a result of changes in the tax law, not the pension laws of 2001. Specifically, amendments to the *Corporate Tax Act* in July 2002 require companies with 300 or more employees to fund any outstanding tax-favored BRP reserves within 4 years; companies with fewer than 300 employees are allowed up to 10 years to fund these reserves (Dai-ichi 2006). According to some pension experts, BRP plans remain a popular employee retirement benefit despite the loss of their tax advantages (Fujiwara 2003 and 2006).

Data in Table 6 indicate there were 992 new DB plan types in operation by 2004, including 479 contract DB plans and 513 fund DB plans, covering 1.35 million workers. By 2006, the number of employees in these new plans exceeded 3.80 million. Approximately 40 percent of all new DB plans operating in June 2005 were cash balance plans, which often cover several companies (Sugita 2006).

The number of corporate DC plans reached 2,191 by the end of January 2007, representing more than a 50-percent increase over 2004. Firms with fewer than 300 employees, primarily in retail and other industries with high turnover levels, operate approximately 80 percent of these DC plans (Daily Yomiuri 2006; Huh and McLellan 2007). Nearly 7,300 companies sponsored DC plans at the end of August 2006—an increase of almost 50 percent from a year earlier (Nikkei Report 2006b). According to some pension experts, much of the increase can be explained by the higher limit allowed for tax-advantaged employer contributions to DC plans, effective in October 2004, encouraging companies to convert more of their existing DB plans into DC plans to reduce the volatility from pension liabilities on corporate balance sheets (Huh and McLellan 2007; McLellan 2004). At the end of December 2006, corporate DC plans covered more than 2.1 million employees—nearly 70 percent more than in 2004 (Table 6).

Even though the number of workers participating in DC plans has been growing, they covered less than 3 percent of the entire Japanese labor force in March 2006 (with about 12 percent of active participants in private-sector pension plans), and accounted for roughly 2 percent of all corporate pension assets. Smaller firms tend to join multiemployer DC plans, which are administered by financial companies with the expertise and resources to handle the administrative and recordkeeping responsibilities. Participation by the self-employed and others eligible for DC plans has been negligible, covering only about 70,000 persons in July 2006.

Prospects for Employer-Sponsored Private Retirement Plans

Buoyant financial markets and steady economic growth, averaging more than 2 percent since 2003, marked an end to nearly 15 years of economic stagnation in Japan. Japanese pension funds have benefited from positive investment returns in the improved economic environment (Chart 1), including an average yield in nominal terms of more than 19 percent for company pension funds in 2005 (Nikkei Report 2006a and 2006b). A survey in 2006 of Japanese occupational pension plans found average funding levels have steadily improved in recent years from 62 percent of liabilities funded in 2003, to 83 percent in 2005, and to 96 percent in early 2006 (Pension & Investments 2006b; Greenwich Associates 2006). The improvements in investment performance and plan funding are contributing to an increasingly optimistic outlook among DB and DC pension plan sponsors, according to that survey (Greenwich Associates 2006).

While employers continue to maintain DB plans for most employees, the financial services industry in Japan is projecting significant growth of DC plans in the next several years (Turner 2006; Nomura Research Institute 2006; Pensions & Investments 2006a). Specifically, pension industry experts consider the mandated termination or conversion of TQPPs by 2012 as the primary source of expected DC plan growth. TQPPs, which accounted for roughly 20 percent of the 17.2 trillion yen (US$ 164.7 million) managed pension assets in 2005, are popular among small and midsized companies. For smaller companies that lack the scale and resources required to set up and manage a DB plan, the less onerous TQPP plan regulations have worked well. A recent report by Nomura Research Institute (NRI) indicated that many companies with TQPP plans might convert to DC plans. NRI expects larger companies to select DC plans (often along- side their existing DB plans), while smaller firms with fewer than 300 employees will likely switch to the government-run Mutual Aid Organization for Employees' Retirement Allowances. The NRI estimates that these mandated TQPP conversions could triple DC plan assets over the next 5 years.

MHLW REVIEW

In October 2006, the Ministry of Health, Labor, and Welfare convened a monthly study group to review the corporate pension system every 5 years as required by law. The study group sought to encourage the growth of DC plans and will examine DB plan issues as well. The study group produced its report in July 2007. According to the government, some recommendations for employer-sponsored retirement plans could be implemented as early as 2008.

The study group examined the taxation of DB contributions and the introduction of a guarantee system in case DB pension funds become insolvent (Nikkei Report 2006c). Issues under discussion for DC plans included:[8] permitting employee contributions, increasing contribution limits, and permitting withdrawals from DC accounts before retirement.

Permitting Employee Contributions

The 2001 DC law prohibited employees from contributing to corporate DC plans. In a U.S. 401(k) plan, by comparison, generally, employees (not the employer) choose to participate if a 401(k) plan is offered by the employer, and the employer may contribute, resulting in a larger pool of tax-deferred savings for participating employees. The typical contribution rate for a 401(k) plan participant is 6 percent of salary, with an employer match of 3 percent (U.S. Department of the Treasury 2006; Munnell and Sundén 2006). There is a maximum limit (indexed for inflation) on the total yearly employee pretax salary deferral for 401(k) plans, which was US$15,500 (1,673,931 yen) for 2007, and employees aged 50 or older are allowed additional pretax "catch-up" contributions of US$5,000 (539,931 yen).

Increasing Contribution Limits

Employees may not contribute to DC plans, and employer contributions are currently limited to 276,000 yen (US$2,344) per year on behalf of employees with access to a qualified DB plan and 552,000 yen (US$4,690) per year on behalf of employees without a qualified DB plan. These limitations prevent DC plans from providing a very high level of retirement benefits. According to the Japanese government, the average employer DC plan contribution in early 2006 was about 4 percent of employee salary. By comparison, contribution limits for US 401(k) plans are much higher, as indicated above.[8] In addition, the limitations on Japanese tax-exempt employer contributions discourage many companies from converting more of their entire pension (EPF or TQPP) plan assets into a single DC plan. Similar to the experience in the U.S., employees in large Japanese companies will more likely receive both DB and DC retirement benefits.

Permitting Withdrawals from DC Accounts before Retirement

Existing prohibitions on employee early withdrawals (before age 60) keep the Japanese DC plan account size unavailable to participants until retirement. Despite the potential threat to income adequacy in retirement, a relaxation of these withdrawal rules for accounts with relatively small asset balances is under consideration.

Other Topics being Considered

Other topics under review include increasing the eligibility age for receiving benefits from DC plans from age 60 to age 65 and exploring ways to improve investment education for DC plan participants.

NOTES

Acknowledgments: Although pension data used in this research come from a variety of sources, the Institute of Pension Research database managed by the Nikko Financial Intelligence, Inc. provided a particularly rich source of information. This online database may be accessed at http://www.nikko-fi.co.jp/modules/p. In addition, the help provided by the Japanese External Trade Organization (JETRO) in obtaining data from the Japanese government was a significant contribution toward the completion of this article.

REFERENCES

Arimori, Miki. (2006). *Highlights of results in Japanese pension field 2005. Nikko Financial*. Available at http:// www.Nikko-fi.co.jp/pension. Accessed April 15, 2006.

Clark, Robert. (1991). *Retirement systems in Japan*. Homewood, IL: University of Pennsylvania Press.

Clark, Robert & Olivia Mitchell. (2002). *Strengthening employment-based pensions in Japan*. Pension Research Council Working Paper PRC WP 2002-1.

Dai-ichi Mutual Life Insurance Company. (2006). *IGP country profile: Japan, 2006*. John Hancock Financial Services, International Group Program (IGP).

Daily Yomiuri. (2006). *Defined-contribution pensions top 2 million. 24 September*. Accessed through http://www .FACTIVA.com on September 27, 2006.

Dow Jones International News. (2006). Japan calls for urgent steps to stem population decline. 1 December. Accessed through *http://www. FACTIVA.com* on December 10, 2006.

Endo, Takahiko. (2002). New trends in retirement benefits spell massive change for Japan. *Benefits and Compensation International, 32(5)*, 10–15.

Freshfields Bruckhaus Deringer. (2003). Corporate pension schemes in Japan. Available at http://www.Freshfields .com. Accessed on August 15, 2006.

Fujiwara, Kiyoaki. (2003). *Traditional severance pay plans and new defined contribution plans in Japan*. Unpublished manuscript.

———. Manager, Tax & Accounting Affairs Group, Economic Policy Bureau, Nippon Keidanren. (2006). Discussion with author (August).

Goldman Sachs. (1999). *Unfunded liabilities of Japanese corporate pensions*. Pension Group Services Report.

Greenwich Associates. (2006). Press Release for the *2006Japanese Investment Management Research Study*.

Hewitt Associates. (2002). Corporate pension reform (Japan). *Legislative updates: Asia & Pacific* (May).

———. (2003). New option for plan sponsors to contract into social security (Japan). *Legislative Updates: Asia & Pacific* (April).

Huh, Elmer & Sarah McLellan. (2007). *A tale of two pension reforms: AUS-Japan comparison*. Pension Research Council Working Paper PRC WP 2007-1.

Japan Ministry of Health, Labor & Welfare. (2003). *White Paper FY2002*.

———. (2004). *Total Research of Labor Conditions in 2003*. ———. 2005a. White Paper FY2004.

———. (2005b). *Textbook for the study programme for the senior social insurance administrators* (Chapter 9). MHLW: Social Insurance Agency.

Kabe, Tetsuo. Counselor, Finance Section, Embassy of Japan. (2006). In discussion with author (May).

Katsumata, Yukiko. (2005). The relationship between the role of the corporate pension and the public pension plan in Japan. In *Rethinking the welfare state: The political economy of pension reform* edited by Martin Rein and Winfried Schmahl. Cheltenham, UK: Edward Elgar.

McGuinness, Fergal. (2003). Sitting and waiting for death and other pension-related issues in Japan. *Benefits and Compensation International, 33(4)*, 3-7.

McLellan, Sarah. (2004). Corporate pension reform in Japan: Big bang or big bust? Pension Research Council Working Paper PRC WP 2004-05.

———. (2005). Corporate pension reform in Japan: Big bangor big bust?

Benefits Quarterly First Quarter: 31-41.

Mizuho Financial Group (MHFG). (2001). Corporate pension funds in Japan. MHFG Fixed Income Research Department. Available at http://www.mizuho-sc.com. Accessed on September 20, 2005.

Morito, Hideyuki. (2001). *Reconsidering Japanese corporate and personal pensions: From a legal point of view*. Organisation for Economic Cooperation and Development.

Munnell, Alicia & Annika Sundén. (2006). 401(k) plans are still coming up short. Center for Retirement Research at Boston College. Issue Brief 43 (March).

Nakada, Tadashi. (2004). Recent corporate pensions reform and its consequences in Japan. Paper presented at the annual PBSS and IAAust Colloqium in Sydney on October 31–November 5, 2004.

Nakamoto, Michiyo. (2003). Japanese pension funds act. *Financial Times*, 27 February.

Nikkei Report. (2006a). Economic rebound lifted corporate pension fund returns 19 percent in FY 05. 7 April. Accessed through http://www.FACTIVA.com on April 10, 2006.

———. (2006b). *Participants in Japan 401(k) plans set to top 2 million*. 17 August. Accessed through http://www .FACTIVA.com on August 22, 2006.

———. (2006c). *Welfare ministry to embark on corporate pension reform*. 7 October. Accessed through http://www .FACTIVA.com on September 10, 2006.

Nomura Research Institute (NRI). (2006). *Japan's Asset Management Business*. Japan: NRI.

Pension Fund Association. (1975-2006). *Annual reports of employees' pension funds*. Japan: Pension Fund Association.

———. (1975-2004). *The basic statistics about companypension plans*. Japan: Pension Fund Association.

Pensions & Investments. (2006a). Japanese DC prepares fortakeoff. 13 November. Accessed November 26, 2006.

———. (2006b). Japan Looking Forward to the Future. 27 November. Accessed November 27, 2006.

Sakamoto, Junichi. (2005). *Japan's pension reform*. World Bank Pension Reform Primer Series.

Sato, Michio. (2005). 2007 problems' loom large. *Daily Yomiuri*. 30 July. Accessed August 5, 2005.

Shimada, Tooru, Satoshi Sugita, Tadanori Chiba & Jumpei Saino. (2002). *New movements in the Japanese corporate pension system*. Paper presented at the XXVIIth International Congress of Actuaries in Mexico.

Shimizu, Nobuhiru. (2005). *Protection of participants and the pension benefit guarantee program of Japan*. Paper presented at the annual OECD/IOP Conference on Private Pensions in Bangkok, Thailand on April 27–28, 2005.

Sugita, Satoshi. (2006). *Plan design and investment policy of cash balance pension plans in Japan*. Paper presented at the 28th International Congress of Actuaries in Paris on May 28–June 2, 2006.

Takahashi, Hiroyuki. (2006). *Visiting Researcher at Employee Benefit* Research Institute, International Affairs Division at Japan MHLW. Discussion with author (September).

Takayama, Noriyuki. (2005). Pension Reform in Japan. Paper presented at the KDI International Conference on Aging in Seoul, Korea on March 17–18, 2005.

Turner, David. (2006). US-Style pension plans popular in Japan. *Financial Times*. 6 February.

Turner, John & David Rajnes. (1995). Pay or Play Pensions in Japan and the United Kingdom. In *Social Security: Time for a Change* edited by Kevin Stephenson. Greenwich, CT: JAI Press, Inc.

U.S. Department of Labor, Bureau of Labor Statistics [BLS]. (2007). *International comparisons of hourly compensation costs for production workers in manufacturing, supplementary tables*. http://www.bls.gov/fls/hcompsupptabtoc.htm. Accessed January 29, 2007.

U.S. Department of the Treasury, Internal Revenue Service. (2006). *IRS announces pension plan limitations for 2007*, IRS Newswire IR-2006-162. October 18, 2006. Accessed July 5, 2007.

U.S. Social Security Administration. (2007). *Social Security Programs Throughout the World: Asia and the Pacific*, 2006. Washington, DC: Office of Policy.

Urata, Haruka. (2001). New developments in corporate pension schemes in Japan. Paper presented at the Project on Intergenerational Equity at the Hitotsubashi University.

Usuki, Masaharu. (2003). Pension funds and retirement benefits in the depressed economy and market: Experience and challenges in Japan. Paper presented at the Eleventh Annual Superannuation Colloqium in Wales, July 2003.

Watanabe, Noriyasu. (1996). Private pension plans in Japan. In *Securing employer-based pensions: An international perspective* edited by Zvi

Bodie et al. Philadelphia: University of Pennsylania Press.

———. (1998). Special topic-Occupational pension systems in Japan. *Japan Labor, 37(8)*.

Watanabe, Yumiko. (Director, Pension and Welfare Department, Japan External Trade Organization). (2006–2007). Discussion with author (September 2006–May 2007).

Yamamoto, Katsuyama & Tetsuo Fukawa. (2003). *The future prospects of Japanese employees pension insurance*. Paper presented at the Fourth International Research Conference on Social Security in Antwerp, Belgium, May 5–7, 2003.

Yermo, Juan. (2002). *Revised taxonomy for pension plans, pension funds, and pension entities*. Organisation for Economic Cooperation and Development.

End Notes

[1] According to provisions of the 2004 social security reform law, the government subsidy for the NP will rise to 50 percent by 2009 (Sakamoto 2005).

[2] The Japanese government uses a male employee and non-working spouse as the model household when publishing the average EPI replacement rate. The current average EPI replacement rate for a female employee is approximately 53 percent, which will decline to 45 percent by 2025. This higher EPI replacement rate for women reflects a lower average wage, versus male workers, and the redistributive benefit formula (Y. Watanabe 2006–2007).

[3] In general, book reserves occur when a voluntary retirement plan's assets are recorded as a liability on the plan sponsor's balance sheet (Yermo 2002).

[4] According to the 2004 social security reform, EPF plans established on or after April 1, 2005, must provide a supplemental benefit equal to 50 percent. However, no EPF plans have been established since April 1, 2005. EPF plans established before April 2005 are not subject to this new rule (Y. Watanabe 2006–2007).

[5] There is an upper limit to the benefit guaranteed by the PFA. If an EPF supplemental benefit is more than 30 percent above the earnings-related EPI benefit replaced, then the guarantee covers 50 percent of the benefit beyond the supplemental 30 percent. A PFA review committee, however, may reduce this extra guaranteed amount for EPF rule violations, such as the failure by trustees to exercise their fiduciary duties. EPF plans support this guarantee system through fees based on the number of plan participants (Clark 1991; Y. Watanabe 2006–2007).

[6] Accounting changes introduced in 2000 did encourage corporations to use market valuation rather than book value to account for pension assets in financial statements. However, the time at which changes in asset values began to be reflected on plan sponsor financial statements was not clear given the continued weakness of financial markets until 2003.

[7] Tables 5 does not show trends in BRP plans. Anecdotal evidence suggests a decline in their use, primarily conversions into newer DB and DC plan types, following the loss of tax advantages in 2002. There are no official figures documenting this decline, however.

[8] This comparison between Japanese and American workers is fair, given that the 2005 hourly compensation costs for production workers in manufacturing are comparable in the two countries: U.S. workers received $23.65 versus Japanese workers received $21.76 (US Bureau of Labor Statistics 2006).

Chapter Sources

The following chapters have been previously published:

Chapter 1 – This is an edited, excerpted and augmented edition of a United States Congressional Research Service publication, Report Order Code R41009, dated January 11, 2010.

Chapter 2 – This is an edited, excerpted and augmented edition of a United States Social Security Adminisration publication.

Chapter 3 – This is an edited, excerpted and augmented edition of a United States Social Security Administration publication, Report Order Code Volume 68 No. 2, dated 2008.

Chapter 4 – This is an edited, excerpted and augmented edition of a United States Social Security Administration publication, Report Order Code Volume 68 No. 2, dated 2008.

Chapter 5 – This is an edited, excerpted and augmented edition of a United States Social Security Administration publication, Report Order Code Volume 67 No. 4, dated 2007.

Chapter 6 – This is an edited, excerpted and augmented edition of a United States Social Security Administration publication, Report Order Code Volume 67 No. 3, dated 2007.

INDEX

D

E

J

K

L

M

N

O

P

R

S